# Jackie's Newport

# Jackie's Newport

## AMERICA'S FIRST LADY and the City by the Sea

Raymond Sinibaldi

Globe Pequot
Guilford, Connecticut

Globe Pequot

An imprint of The Rowman & Littlefield Publishing Group, Inc.
4501 Forbes Blvd., Ste. 200
Lanham, MD 20706
www.rowman.com

Distributed by NATIONAL BOOK NETWORK



Photos courtesy of: The JFK Library; JFK Library Toni Frissell Collection; JFK Library White House Photographers Robert Knudsen, Abbie Rowe and Cecil Stoughton; The Associated Press; *Fort Worth Star-Telegram* Collection; Special Collections, The University of Texas at Arlington Library, Arlington, Texas; Newscom Services, Inc., Stan Stearns



British Library Cataloguing in Publication Information available

**Library of Congress Cataloging-in-Publication Data available**

ISBN 978-1-4930-3654-7 (paperback)
ISBN 978-1-4930-3655-4 (e-book)

™ The paper used in this publication meets the minimum requirements of American National Standard for Information Sciences—Permanence of Paper for Printed Library Materials, ANSI/NISO Z39.48-1992

Printed in the United States of America

To Nancy Marie Sinibaldi Cappellini, the very best of us . . .

*Our Connection is pure love.*

# Contents

# Author's Note

I dare say no biographer will ever truly come to know Jackie, a passionately private person. She saved that for those whom she treasured and loved. It is my hope that these pages will bring you a greater understanding of the challenges she faced, the strength and resiliency it took to simply endure and the depth of character exhibited while doing so. I hope this will bring a deeper perspective of the toughness and inner strength she carried within that slender frame and behind her soft whispery voice.

To those of you who met Jackie only in later books and media, it is my hope that you will come to a deeper appreciation and understanding of her triumphs, her tragedies, what she means to this country and why she still resonates today.

For those of you who lived in the times in which she lived, you will find within these pages a window to them. You are about to journey to a bygone American era, when televisions first began bringing America's leaders into America's homes. When John F. Kennedy was sworn in to his first term in Congress there were 44,000 television sets in the country, and fifteen years later that number grew to over 67,000,000. There were no DVRs and certainly no remotes. Phones were dialed and usually hung on kitchen walls. Rhythm and blues and rock and roll were born, and Elvis's gyrating hips were censored off television. Rap was a sheet one acquired upon being arrested, and hip hop was something Peter Cottontail did on the bunny trail. Baseball and boxing dominated the sports world.

The end of World War II ushered in the Cold War. The arms race raged, the space race dawned, and the Civil Rights Movement refused to be denied. Only 20 percent of Americans graduated college, of which only 5 percent were women who comprised but 20 percent of the work force.

It was in this cauldron of simplicity and tumult that Jack and Jackie Kennedy emerged. Glamorous, dashing, and young, they changed the face of the American political landscape: she, a uniquely beautiful Newport socialite, and he a war hero. She was thirty-one when she became the first lady, the third youngest wife of a president, and only thirty-four when she led the nation through the horrors of that November weekend in 1963.

Remember, as you take this journey into the past, that the hard drives of bygone eras do not contain the same computer chips of today. Chips are added, chips are deleted as society and culture evolves. History itself is a living, breathing entity, to be evaluated without judgement, but in the knowledge that there remains a universality among people, crossing all the professed barriers of race, age, religion, economic station, ethnicity, sexual orientation or political affiliation and which is best articulated in Jackie's own words.

"Even though people may be well known, they still hold in their hearts the emotions of a simple person, for the moments that are most important of those we know on earth…birth, marriage and death."

*Raymond Sinibaldi*
*December 2018*

## PART I

# Jackie, Newport and Hammersmith Farm

> "We both went bareback riding in a field in Newport on two unbroken horses."
>
> Jacqueline Kennedy

These last bitter days we have had a queen. She came to us, not by heredity or coronation, but by marriage to our president and by the chrism of sorrow and the grace of God. With majestic pace and instant dignity, she disciplined our grief, made us proud in our shame, and gave us gentle strength to nurture future Americans. Every woman has a new grace, every wife a new radiance, every mother a new tender courage.

Our gratitude shall make us better men, more appreciative husbands and more responsible fathers. But above all, women and men alike we shall walk with more erect humility, in the way of restrained freedom, forgiving justice and untarnished peace."

Thus wrote Albert T. Mollegan, professor at the Virginia Theological Seminary, to the *Washington Post* just three days after Jackie Kennedy laid her husband to rest in Arlington National Cemetery. Embodied within lay the elucidation of how Jacqueline Lee Bouvier Kennedy seized the soul of her country and captured the hearts of the world.

When history's cruel hand struck her, she persevered through its horror, bringing sense and sensibility to the chaos of madness. With a combined sense of duty, loyalty, determination, and self-preservation, she set forth to create and preserve Jack's legacy, in which she now shares.

Jacqueline Lee Bouvier arrived in Newport in June 1942, one month shy of her thirteenth birthday, a sudden upheaval brought on by her mother Janet's marriage to Hugh D. Auchincloss Jr. Jackie and her sister, Lee, four years younger, were visiting their grandfather when a phone call came. "She's gotten married," Jackie said to Lee. "To Mr. Auchincloss."[1]

The twisted and tangled web that blended the families Auchincloss and Bouvier began in the waning summer days of the late nineteenth century. Hugh Dudley Auchincloss Jr. was born at Hammersmith Farm on August 15, 1897. One week later, nearly 700 visitors "were taken around the Ocean Drive," making a stop at "the Auchincloss place 'Hammersmith Farm'... Where the fine view of the bay and harbor was heartily appreciated by the strangers."[2] Unbeknownst to any of those strangers, inside lay a new baby boy who would become the conduit that would bring to Newport one of the world's most admired women of the twentieth century.

Hugh married three times. The first, to Russian noblewoman Maya Chrapovitsky, produced Hugh Dudley Auchincloss III. He came to be called Yusha, and he was the Auchincloss to whom Jackie was the closest. Yusha grew to become an expert on Middle Eastern affairs and, in that capacity, worked as an unofficial, unpaid advisor to JFK during his presidency. In 1935, Hugh married again, this time to divorced socialite and Broadway

Jackie with Janet Lee Bouvier at the East Hampton Long Island Fair in July of 1935. Jackie followed in her mother's footsteps becoming an award winning equestrian.

actress Nina Gore Vidal. She brought a son, Gore, to the union, which ended in 1941 after producing a daughter, Nina, and another son, Thomas.

New York socialite and nationally known equestrian Janet Thornton Lee married fellow socialite and Wall Street broker John Vernon Bouvier III in 1928. Known as "Black Jack" for his perpetual tan and swashbuckling, extravagant ways, his drinking, gambling, and philandering would lead to divorce in 1940. That was not, however, before the birth of two daughters, Jacqueline Lee and Caroline Lee. Janet and Black Jack's bitter divorce would leave Jackie and Caroline, called Lee, in the crossfire of their parents' personal war throughout their lives.

Hammersmith Farm suited Jackie well. Perched above Narragansett Bay, it satisfied a calling she'd always heard from the sea and one she answered with a poem, written and illustrated at the age of ten, about summers and the sea on the beaches of the Hamptons.

**Sea Joy**

When I go down by the sandy shore
I can think of nothing I want more
Than to live by the blooming blue sea
As the seagulls flutter round about me

I can run about-when the tide is out
With the wind and the sand and the sea all about
And the seagulls are swirling and diving for fish
Oh-to live by the sea is my only wish.
Me 1939 [3]

As Jackie was familiarizing herself with her new summer home, just across Narragansett Bay John F. Kennedy was instructing young naval officers on the finer points of PT boat command. World War II was raging, and Jackie became ensconced in it as much as a thirteen-year-old girl could be. Uncle Hughdie, as she would come to call her stepfather, reopened

Jackie, atop her Piebald pony Dance Step, receives her winner's cup for the nine and under division at the East Hampton Horseshow in August 1937.

Hammersmith as a working farm with the purchase of two Guernsey cows. He named them Jacqueline and Caroline. The ninety acres of green fields once again produced food supplies, this time for the U.S. Navy. Jackie's chore was tending to more than two thousand Rhode Island Red hens.

For the three remaining summers of World War II, Jackie shared Hammersmith with her stepbrothers Yusha and Thomas and stepsister, Nina. Half-sister Janet joined the fray in 1945, with half-brother Jamie rounding out the family two years later, leaving Jackie's sibling tally at six. To the credit of all, they never considered themselves as step or halves, only brothers and sisters. Jackie's room was on the third floor with a large window overlooking the lawn, the woods, and the river.

Jackie's winters were spent in McLean, Virginia, on the Auchincloss Merrywood Estate. The eleven-bedroom, 23,000-square-foot mansion perched on fifty acres overlooking the Potomac River was only eight miles from downtown Washington, D.C. Jackie found solace and joy in both places. "I always love it so at Merrywood," she wrote to Yusha. "So peaceful, with the river and the dogs, listening to the Victrola…I will never know which I love best, Hammersmith with its green fields and summer winds or Merrywood in the snow with the river and those great steep hills."[4]

Both homes provided comfort even when away from them. While traveling in Italy Jackie wrote to Hughdie, "I began to feel terribly homesick as I was driving…I started thinking of things like the path leading to the stable at Merrywood…and Hammersmith with the foghorns blowing at night…all the places…that bind you to a family you love…you take with you, no matter how far you go."[5]

Jackie was dichotomous, cut from a different cloth, alternately lamenting her conviction that "no one will ever marry me and I'll end up a housemother at Farmington,"[6] whilst writing in her Farmington yearbook that her ambition in life was "not to be a housewife."

"To meet her, even during those adolescent years, was never to forget her," remembered Letitia Baldridge, who became Jackie's White House social secretary. "She was a natural beauty wearing none of the teenage cosmetic fashions of the day." What captivated Baldridge the most was "her voice…unforgettable in its soft breathy tones…a sound that forced you to draw close and listen well."[7]

Some contemporaries were critical within their complimentary observations. "A little bit too well dressed," observed Priscilla McMillan upon seeing her for the first time at a debutante party on Long Island. "She was stylish even though she was only sixteen." Apparently too stylish for McMillan's tastes. "If you were really upper draw," she continued, "You might be pretty and...well dressed...not glamorous and socially precocious. You were just well bred and nice...you didn't necessarily have clusters and clusters of boys around you."[8] Jackie did, though. "She was the center of attention even then and of course it made the other girls quite jealous."[9]

Selwa "Lucky" Roosevelt, a Vassar classmate, observed Jackie's dichotomy, recalling "an almost star like quality...when she entered a room you couldn't help but notice her, she was such an exquisite creature..." and yet "she seemed so private."[10]

"I remember seeing her once as a debutant," recalled Newport contemporary Susan Neuberger Wilson. "I remember catching my breath... as she walked down a flight of stairs...she was so regal...I've never forgotten that moment."[11]

Columbus O'Donnell, another Newport acquaintance, remembered her as "a bit standoffish...[not] a bubbling teenager by any means...very bright...interested in her family and books and more serious things than just going out on dates." An Auchincloss cousin recalled, "I would have preferred a little less seriousness and a little more partying."[12]

"Miss Bouvier's coming out party took the form of a reception and dance...at Hammersmith Farm" on Thursday afternoon, August 7, 1947.[13] Eight days later a party followed at the Clambake Club, where Jackie was joined by Rose Grosvenor and presented to Newport society. In reporting, Nancy Randolph captured the dichotomy of Newport itself: "There are estates magnificent enough to jolt a maharajah; others weed grown, closed and clammy enough to attract ghosts. And like the houses the people, some brilliantly decorating the social scene on lawns and sand...others walking Bellevue Ave in solitary out of date grandeur, in clothes more in the style of the Smithsonian Institute than Schiaparelli."[14]

Jackie was not a stranger to the social pages of newspapers. She made her first appearance at the top of the Brooklyn Eagle Society page in December 1929 at five months of age. Throughout her young life, her equestrian exploits were chronicled as she, like her mother, became a highly accomplished horsewoman. However, her appearance in Cholly Knickerbocker's nationally syndicated column in January 1947 established a new paradigm on par with Hollywood starlets.

For the first time since the inception of World War II, the society pages resumed their tradition of naming Queen Debutant of the Year. The 1947 winner was Vassar freshman Jacqueline Bouvier, "a regal brunette who has classic features and the daintiness of Dresden porcelain [with] all the poise, soft-spoken-ness and intelligence that the leading debutante should have. You don't have to read a batch of press clippings to notice her qualities."[15]

Her passion for "serious things" did not preclude her propensity for boys, but it was older boys who held her interest. One in particular was twenty-four-year-old Charles Whitehouse. An American born in Paris, Charles's family summered at Newport's Eastbourne Lodge. Eight years Jackie's senior, his studies at Yale were interrupted by World War II, after which he returned to Yale, Newport, and his horses. "Jackie was crazy about Charlie," said his cousin Susan Alsop. "Charlie was a great horseman, which made him even more attractive to Jackie."[16] Whitehouse remembered she was as "brave as a lioness" on the back of a horse.[17] Following Jackie's coming out, they spent considerable time together. "We were very fond of each other," he recalled, "and that fondness continued over the years."[18]

College, Europe, a career, and marriage all lay before Jackie. The particulars of each were just waiting to be chosen.

Charlie Bartlett first met Jack Kennedy in 1940, when he accompanied a mutual friend to supper at the Kennedy home in Hyannis Port. They became friends and then political associates when Bartlett was appointed the Washington correspondent for the *Chattanooga Times* in 1948. He also knew Jacqueline Bouvier, having met her in Easthampton. "An enormously attractive girl…she used to go up and visit with her father in the summer.

She always had these sort of English beaus and I must say they were not up to her."[19] Bartlett donned the role of Cupid at his brother's wedding in Long Island in 1948. Both Jackie and Jack were guests, and Bartlett attempted to introduce them. However, when escorting Jackie across the crowded ballroom, they encountered former heavyweight boxing champ Gene Tunney. A conversation ensued, and by the time they made it across the hall, Congressman Kennedy had left.

The following summer Jackie was bound for Paris and the Sorbonne for her junior year of college and an experience unlike any she'd known. One of five students staying in a one-bathroom flat, where the heat and hot water often did not work, she donned winter clothes to go to bed. She spent a year floating between the worlds of Bohemian college student and socialite, moving from the evocative cafes and clubs of Paris's Left Bank to dinners at the Ritz; from third-class train rides, where young ladies armed themselves with hatpins to ward off gropers, to riding horses; and from water closets, where a lady need stand to accomplish the objective, using newspaper when finished, to afternoons exploring the Louvre.

Sparing the vagaries of the Bohemian aspects of her world, Jackie frequently wrote to her mother, explaining to Yusha, "I have to write mummy a ream each week, or she gets hysterical and thinks I'm dead or married to an Italian." [20] Classes ended, and Jackie spent her summer on a third-class train tour through Germany and Austria, visiting Dachau and Berchtesgaden (Hitler's Eagle's Nest). Yusha joined her for three weeks in Scotland and Ireland. In Dublin, Jackie met Father Joseph Leonard of All Hallows College. Leonard, an old friend of Jackie's step-uncle, met them at Dublin Airport and chaperoned them about Ireland.[21] "She loved the stories about the kings and castles in Ireland," recalled Yusha, adding, "She had a wonderful series of conversations with [Father Leonard] and then came back to America and got into a correspondence." A friendship was forged, and the seventy-three-year-old priest became friend, mentor, pen pal, and confidant to the twenty-one-year-old socialite. Their relationship lasted until Leonard's death in 1964.

It was the spring of 1951 when Bartlett, now married, attempted to play Cupid again, this time at a small dinner party at the Bartletts' Georgetown home. Dinner was followed by a game of charades in which Jackie and Jack were paired. Jackie, who had scheduled a date for later in the evening, departed early and was escorted to her car by Charlie. Jack, obviously interested, followed them outside. "Jackie, can I take you someplace to have a drink?" [22] he asked, only to be interrupted by Bartlett's dogs yipping at someone in the backseat of Jackie's convertible.

"Maybe some other time," came Jackie's reply, leaving Jack speechless.[23]

"Some other time" arrived, but not before Jackie had obtained her BA degree in French literature from George Washington University, procured a position as the Inquiring Camera Girl with the *Washington Times Herald*, and become engaged then unengaged in a three-month span.

When Jackie graduated college in 1951, she was one of only 5 percent of American women to possess a college degree. Creeping up on twenty-two years of age, and having lived abroad for a year, she longed for independence. For 80 percent of American women, this meant marriage, and in the United States in 1950, the average age at which women married was twenty years and four months.[24] Jackie was deemed, by many, to be rapidly heading toward spinsterhood. Following another European summer sojourn, this one with her sister Lee, Jackie's mother urged her to settle down and get married.

Jackie met John Husted at a Washington party, introduced by Yusha's girlfriend at the time. There are varying accounts of the aborted engagement. Some have Janet initially on board with the marriage and then torpedoing it upon learning that Husted's finances and those of his family were not sufficient. Some have Charlie and Martha Bartlett ignoring the engagement and working behind the scenes in continued efforts to bring Jack and Jackie together. The details notwithstanding, the fact is that the engagement came to an end, with Jackie slipping the ring into Husted's pocket after driving him to the airport following a weekend visit to Virginia. The engagement announcement on January 21, 1952, called for a June wedding. On March 22, it had been "terminated by mutual consent." [25] Jackie wrote to her friend:

> *Dearest Father Leonard,*
> *Such a long silence from me—it wasn't a very happy time, and I guess that's why I haven't written you. I was going to explain it to you—but once it had calmed down, I hated the thought of hashing it all over again. I know it's for the best now and I have learned so much from this—but it seems ashamed comment on my maturity that I had to learn the thing you look for to build a life together on, this way. I'm ashamed that we both went into it so quickly and gaily but I think the suffering it brought us both for a while afterwards, was the best thing—we both needed something of a shock to make us grow up. I don't know if John has—I haven't seen him and I don't really want to, not out of meanness—it's just better if that all dies away and we forget we knew each other—but I know it's grown me up and it's about time! The next time will be ALL RIGHT and have a happy ending— So much love to you*
>
> *-Jacqueline*

Holding another dinner party in May 1952, Martha Bartlett called Jackie, extending an invitation along with a suggestion that she invite Congressman Kennedy, who had just announced his intent to run for the Senate. The cosmic tumblers now in place, the two clicked, and Jackie "knew instantly that he would have a profound, perhaps disturbing, influence on her life. She was frightened…in this self-revealing moment envisaged heartbreak, but just as swiftly determined such heartbreak would be worth the pain." [26]

"Do you want to know something strange" she wrote to Leonard. "Whenever I think about something a lot, I always want to share it with you. What a buildup, it isn't even all that earth shaking. It's just who I think I'm in love with and I think it would interest you, John Kennedy." She also expressed the source of her fear: "He's like my father in a way...Loves the chase and is bored with the conquest, and once married, needs proof he's still attractive so flirts with other women and resents you. I saw how that nearly killed mummy." [27]

Jack and Jackie had a lot in common. Both were exceedingly well read and possessive of a sardonic wit paired with a dark sense of humor. They shared a passion for history and literature and found the same heroes in both realms. Among them were Winston Churchill[28] and British Romantic poet Lord Byron. [29] They also shared a stoic demeanor, carrying their burdens with a quiet dignity. "They were two lonely people," noted writer and friend Charles Spaulding, "and they instantly recognized that in each other. Jackie, often happiest in solitary pursuits, horseback riding or simply reading. Jack, incessantly reading and beneath his steel exterior, Jackie saw 'this lonely sick little boy...in bed so much of the time reading history, devouring the Knights of the Round Table.'" [30]

Jack's interest and curiosity were piqued at their first meeting and soon blossomed into an immediate yearning. "My brother was really smitten with her...from the very beginning," noted youngest brother Teddy, adding, "He was fascinated by her intelligence." [31]

"From that point on," said Bartlett, "this thing was pretty well moving along...to the priest." [32]

Jackie had officially entered the world of journalism as the *Washington Herald*'s Inquiring Camera Girl, equipped with her own byline. She now found herself hitting the streets of Washington armed with questions for the populace. Many related to love, marriage, and politics. Some were poignantly prophetic: "Which first lady would you like to have been?" "What prominent person's death affected you most?" Some would never be asked today: "Noel

Jack and his young sister-in-law Janet Auchincloss chatting on the lawn at Hammersmith Farm.

Coward [33] said, 'Some woman should be struck regularly like gongs.' What do you think?" "Chaucer[34] said, 'What women most desire is power over men.' What do you think women desire most?" And some pertained to Jackie: "Should a candidate's wife campaign with her husband?"

Jack and Jackie began dating regularly, though not exclusively. They mostly attended small dinner parties, often at the Bartletts, followed by games of bridge, Chinese checkers, Monopoly or charades. Jack was immersed in his campaign for the Senate, which ultimately ended in victory. After assuming his Senate seat in January 1953, Jack proposed to Jackie in May, but the engagement announcement was delayed. There were two national publications doing stories on the newly elected senator from Massachusetts, the country's most eligible bachelor, and Jackie was bound for England to cover the coronation of Queen Elizabeth II.

While in England, Jackie received a wire from Jack. "Article's excellent, but you are missed," he wrote in a rare romantic gesture, following it with a transatlantic phone call.[35] Jackie, meanwhile collected some out-of-print books to bring home to Jack, and when she landed in Boston, he greeted her at the airport. The first person to learn of the engagement was Jackie's Aunt Maud. Jackie called her aunt from the airport. "Aunt Maudie," she said, "I'm engaged to Jack Kennedy...but you can't tell anyone for a while... it wouldn't be fair to the *Saturday Evening Post*...[It's] coming out tomorrow with an article...the title...Jack Kennedy—The Senate's Gay Young Bachelor."[36] There was one more person Jackie wanted to contact before the official release hit the news. She wired Father Leonard: "ANNOUNCING ENGAGEMENT TO JACK KENNEDY TOMORROW, LETTER FOLLOWS, SO HAPPY, LOVE JACQUELINE."[37] The following day newspapers across the country announced that America's most eligible bachelor was ineligible: "Newport Colonist, Senator John Kennedy to Be Wed Here in September,"[38] read the hometown news.

Throughout her young life, Jackie wrote. There were birthday poems to family and friends. Poems of life and her place in it. Imaginary tales of all the pets in her life and her satirical future predictions about members of her family. For herself she envisioned "the circus queen who, though admired by the world's biggies, married the man in the flying trapeze."[39]

There was less than three months until the wedding, and the unification of the families was on a collision course. The East Coast hunting set of New

York and Newport and the rough-and-tumble, fast-living Irish Kennedy clan had differing views of style, taste, propriety, and decorum. Janet reached out to Rose Kennedy with an invitation to come to Newport for lunch to discuss wedding plans. Jack and Jackie joined Rose and Janet for lunch as Janet made her intentions and expectations clear: a small affair, very exclusive, with a few close family and friends. She saw no need nor desire for the press, photographers, or crowds; a simple notice in the Newport and Washington newspapers would announce the marriage. "Look, Mrs. Auchincloss," said Jack, "your daughter is marrying...a senator...who may one day be president. There are going to be photographers whether we like it or not. So the idea is to show Jackie to best advantage."[40]

The first round of the collision was a draw, leading to the arrival of Papa Joe Kennedy the following weekend. This meeting personified the differences embodied in their two worlds: the staid socialite mom and the rough, driven Irish politician dad. The combination of Joe Kennedy's powerful personality and boundless wealth steamrolled Janet. The result was that St. Mary's Church of Newport would be filled to capacity, and 1,400 guests would gather on the Hammersmith lawn to celebrate the wedding of Jackie and Jack.

The Kennedys applied the same brashness with which they took on Senator Henry Cabot Lodge and the Boston Brahmins in the 1952 election, for to Joe, the old New York/Newport socialites were the same. "They don't know how to live up there in Newport," Joe told Red Fay.[41] "Their wealth is from a bygone era. Most of them are just keeping up a front and owe everybody...I tell you they don't know the first thing about living up there as compared to the way we live down here."[42]

Charles Whitehouse observed, "There was no push for success from Mr. and Mrs. Auchincloss and all that was quite different from the hard drive for success...that Mr. Kennedy was imbuing in his children." It left the older families of Newport and New York to view the Kennedys "with some questioning." Pausing, he added, "To put it politely."[43]

The best or worst manifestation of the collision between the Kennedy culture and that of Newport played out at the bachelor's dinner at Newport's Clambake Club. Jack consulted his married buddy "Red" Fay about the protocol of toasting his bride. Fay related to him the tradition of the toast to the bride, which ended with the glass thrown into the fireplace and broken out of respect.

The problem was that Fay had conflated the idea of the Jewish tradition with Emily Post's etiquette. Emily Post wrote, "The breaking habit originated with drinking to the bride's health and breaking the stem of the wine glass, so that it might never serve a less honorable purpose." After the groom rises, his glass filled with champagne, he offers it to the bride, and then "every man rises, drinks the toast standing, and then breaks the delicate stem of the glass. [44] Post's tradition was specifically for the bachelor's party. The ancient Jewish custom follows that after the groom has toasted his bride at their wedding, he throws his glass, breaking it against the northern wall of the room. This serves a twofold purpose, as noise is said to ward off evil spirits believed to invade from the north.

With the dinner drawing to a close, Jack stood, and the other seventeen men present stood with him. Raising their Chrystal glasses, heirlooms of the Auchincloss family, Fay recalled that Jack began, "To my future bride Jackie. We will not drink from this glass again out of respect for my future bride." Jack fired first, and then sixteen glasses followed, crashing in the fireplace. Hugh Auchincloss held on to his. The evening progressed, the glasses were replaced, and Jack—apparently deeply moved by the occasion and tradition—rose again. "I'm so moved," he said, "another toast to my bride." And seventeen more glasses met their fate in the Clambake's fireplace. They drank the rest of the night from glasses that appeared to come from the local diner. [45]

The crowd began to gather early on Saturday morning, September 12, 1953, as residents wanted to catch a glimpse of "Newport's most brilliant wedding in many years." The church could accommodate but half of the 1,400 invited guests, requiring special passes for entry. The others would gather for the post-nuptial reception under tents spread across the Hammersmith lawn overlooking Narragansett Bay. While guests poured into the city on Friday night, an electrical failure at the Muenchinger-King Hotel had patrons signing in by candlelight, adding to the ambiance of the eve for some.

As "notables from official life, the business world and society looked on...at least 2,000 Newporters turned out to watch, as much as they could, of the year's banner social event." [46] Some of the more daring found their way into the church, sprinkling themselves among guests in the rear pews and the choir loft.

The morning weather was perfect for the perfect bride on her perfect day. However, unbeknownst to Newporters and the on-looking world, the day was anything but perfect. The winds, which picked up off the bay throughout the day, portended the storm brewing between and among Black Jack, Janet, and Jackie.

Black Jack Bouvier had been excluded from the bachelor's party and bridal dinner but was present at the rehearsal in preparation to walk Jackie down the aisle. Before the bridal dinner Janet sent Lee's husband, Michael Canfield, to the Viking Hotel to deliver a message. "He could of course come to the church and give away the bride," Michael said, relaying Janet's words, "but he could not come to the reception." [47] Isolated, alone, and still intent on walking his daughter down the aisle of St. Mary's Church, Black Jack headed straight for the hotel bar and began renewing his "strong alliance with alcohol." [48]

The wedding morn Jackie's twin Bouvier aunts, Maude and Michelle, sent their husbands to the Viking to look in on Black Jack. They found him, half naked, slurring his speech and unable to even stand. The men called and reported his condition. Michelle placed a call to Janet explaining "he had

Jackie with her father John Bouvier at the East Hampton fashion show, July 1949. Jackie was named after the feminine version of her father's nickname, Black Jack.

Jack and Jackie emerge from St. Mary's following their wedding ceremony to the cheers of thousands gathered outside. St. Mary's is the oldest Catholic church in Newport, built by Irish immigrants.

Joe Kennedy plants a kiss on the cheek of his daughter-in-law on her wedding day. Jackie got along famously well with the elder Kennedy. He very much admired her intelligence and independence and she his strength of personality.

The wind off the bay reached 25 miles per hour during the afternoon and wreaked havoc for the photographers. Pausing for a break, Janet holds onto Jackie's dog Soufflé while Jack fixes his hair.

apparently taken a few drinks, but they felt he could pull himself together in time to walk Jackie down the aisle."[49] Janet now had her way: Hugh would walk Jackie down the aisle. "It was the cruelest thing Janet could have done to both Black Jack and Jackie," said Lee, "a sign of the tremendous bitterness she still felt toward him."[50]

The press were told by Joe Kennedy that Mr. Bouvier had taken ill with the flu. Jackie, heartbroken, asked Charles Spaulding if he could "get him into the church."

"We got him into the pew," Spaulding reported, "but it was an interesting maneuver."[51] Jackie carried her disappointment with grace and composure, only weeping when she went to her bedroom to change. She emerged with Jack, smiling and radiant, and was off to New York, then Acapulco, for the honeymoon. After settling in Acapulco, the first thing she did was write her father a long letter filled with love and understanding, telling him that "as far as she was concerned...he was the one who had accompanied her down the aisle."[52]

Jackie embraced her role as the wife of a U.S. senator in a life that proved to be, in her words, "terrifically nomadic."[53] The first order of business occurred when Jackie and Jack returned from their honeymoon. "I was taken immediately to Boston to be registered as a democrat."[54] Her escort was Robert "Patsy" Mulkern. "He took me up and down the street and told me that 'duking' means shaking hands."[55] It was Jackie's introduction to street-level politics 101, and it came at the hands of Patsy, a former prizefighter also known as the "China Doll." Other mentors included "Onions" Burke and "Juicy" Grenara. "Those names just fascinated me so...to...see that world and then go have dinner at the Ritz" brought a laugh to her as she recalled it. It was her first tutorial in moving through the stratum of politics.

As a teenage girl Jackie often pondered the life of a gypsy. She even wrote of it in a poem: "I love the feeling down inside me that says to run away, to come and be a gypsy, and laugh the gypsy way."[56] She could not

Jackie prepares to throw her bridal bouquet down the staircase at Hammersmith Farm. Jackie's lifelong friend Nancy Tuckerman caught the bouquet, and would later serve as her assistant in the White House.

have imagined that as the wife of a U.S. senator she would come to live the nomadic lifestyle of a gypsy. A high-society gypsy but a gypsy nonetheless. "We'd rent, January until June, then we'd go live at my mother's house... in Virginia for the summer...going up to the Cape when we could on weekends—and in the fall we'd stay with his father. And then we'd go to his apartment in Boston, or we'd go to New York for a couple of days...and then we'd go away after Christmas...for a few days. Such a pace...it just seemed like it was suitcases...always moving."[57]

Jack suffered from myriad gastrointestinal and adrenal difficulties throughout his life, all brought on by Addison's disease. The only ailment of which the public was aware was his back, which was attributed to an old football injury, exacerbated by his service in the South Pacific during the war.[58] By 1950 he suffered from chronic backaches caused by the fact that the bones in his spinal column were collapsing. The following year compression fractures appeared in his lower spine, and for the next few years he spent a good deal of time utilizing crutches to walk. "Before we were married," remembered Jackie, "I can remember him on crutches more than not."[59] Relief would come in spurts, and he took advantage of it. "The month before we were married, we both went bareback riding in a field in Newport on two unbroken work horses and galloped all around the golf course."[60] They even played golf on their honeymoon, but the relief was taking longer to arrive and its stay grew shorter. With "Jack...being driven so crazy by his pain,"[61] the talk turned to surgery. It would fuse his spine with a metal plate, yet there were no guarantees that it would even work. "I don't care," said Jack, "I can't go on like this."[62] Two surgeries, in 1954 and 1955, followed. The first fused his spine, and the second removed the plate as it caused infections. Both nearly killed him.

Jackie was at Jack's side even while fighting through struggles of her own. Her fear that Jack was "like my father" proved all too true, and she found coping with his dalliances far more difficult than she had anticipated.

Disappointment that she did not get pregnant right away turned into dismay when she did in 1955, only to miscarry twelve weeks into the pregnancy. At that point she learned that conceiving, carrying, and bearing children could prove difficult for her. To her delight, she became pregnant again and was due in the fall of 1956.

In August Jackie accompanied Jack to the Democratic Convention in Chicago, where he pursued the vice-presidential spot, which Adlai Stevenson threw out for the delegates to choose. At one point needing only thirty-eight votes to grab the nomination, Jack ultimately fell short but unified the convention when he asked them to declare Estes Kefauver as the unanimous choice. His performance launched his national appeal, for despite his defeat, a Boston scribe wrote, "Jack probably rates as the one real victor of the entire convention."[63] His political future never looked brighter.

Exhausted upon their return home, Jack was bound for some fun in the sun, sailing off the coast of France, while Jackie was headed to Hammersmith Farm. Five days later, Jackie lost the baby, a stillborn girl taken by Caesarean section, and Jack was nowhere to be found. It was three days before he returned, and when he did, a chasm had come between them. They sold their new house in Hickory Hill, with its newly added nursery, and rumors of divorce were everywhere. *Time* magazine reported that Joe offered her one million dollars to stay with Jack. Seeing the article, Jackie called Joe and, laughing, asked, "Why not ten million?"[64] There was no truth to the story, and Jackie had no intent on divorcing Jack, but changes were made in their relationship, primarily involving fewer family demands from the Kennedy clan.

The hope of spring brought hope to Jackie when she learned she was pregnant again. The couple finally had a home, which they had purchased in Georgetown, and Jack was laying the groundwork for his presidential bid in 1960. Jack's reelection to the Senate loomed in November 1958, an undertaking that Jackie categorized as a "major frantic effort…that

Wedding guests gather around tables overlooking Narragansett Bay in the background, while two police officers stand near the fence on the left. The guests watched the bride and groom's first dance to the song "I Married an Angel," chosen by Jack.

Reception dinner tables with Hammersmith Farm in the background. The cottage had 28 rooms, 13 bathrooms and 14 fireplaces. The *Newport Daily News* compared the wedding to Vanderbilt and Astor weddings of bygone days.

The newlyweds are captured with Jackie's veil billowing in the wind and Narragansett Bay in the background. Within eight years, the lawn just behind the wooden fence would become the landing zone for Marine I, the presidential helicopter.

Jack and Jackie pose in the water in Acapulco on their honeymoon, mimicking a scene from the movie *From Here to Eternity*, which came out in August 1953. Nominated for 13 Academy Awards, it won eight, including best picture.

campaign was the hardest campaign…ever."[65] However, before that Jackie would be transformed first by a death and then by new life.

It was August 3, and she was six months pregnant, when the call came. Rushing to the Lenox Hill Hospital in Manhattan, with Jack at her side, she arrived minutes too late. Black Jack was gone, a victim of liver cancer at age sixty-six. His "strong alliance with alcohol" had finally done him in. Jackie arranged his funeral service at St. Patrick's Cathedral and his burial in East Hampton. Viewing him for the last time, she removed a bracelet from her wrist and placed it in his hand. It was the bracelet he had given her when she graduated from Farmington.

The day after Thanksgiving, November 27, 1957, Jackie gave birth to a full-term, healthy, seven-pound, two-ounce baby girl. Caroline Bouvier

Kennedy was, according to her father, as "robust as a sumo wrestler."[66] Three weeks later, Jackie returned to St. Patrick's with Caroline, clad in the same dress she herself had worn when Archbishop Richard Cushing of Boston baptized her into the Roman Catholic faith. "As new life will come from death, love will come at leisure. Love of love, love of life and giving without measure, gives in return a wondrous yearn of a promise almost seen. Live hand-in-hand and together we'll stand on the threshold of a dream."[67] The pair now stood on the threshold of their dreams as individuals and as a couple.

The Kennedy siblings serenaded the newlyweds at the head table. Singing was a staple at Kennedy family gatherings. Left to right, Bobby (best man), Patricia (not visible), Eunice, Ted, and Jean. To the right of Jack is Jackie's sister Lee (maid of honor) and mother Janet Auchincloss.

The arrival of Caroline transformed their marriage. The elated couple moved into their new home in Georgetown, finally putting their nomadic life behind them. Jackie went about the business of making her home with a new understanding of her role as the wife of a politician with a newfound hope and a newfound purpose. "I wouldn't say that being married to a busy politician is the easiest life to adjust to," she told one reporter. "But...you figure out the best way to do things—to keep the house running smoothly, to spend as much time as you can with your husband and your children—and eventually you'll find yourself well adjusted...The most important thing for a successful marriage is for a husband to do what he likes best and does well, the wife's satisfaction will follow."[68]

Shortly after Jack's death she talked of him and the people in his life. "He loved us all," she said, from the "people in the three-deckers" to those with whom he walked the halls of the White House. He loved "Kenny[69] and Dave[70], and you [Arthur Schlesinger][71] and Ken Galbraith[72]." He loved "the Irish and his family...He loved me and my sister in the world that had nothing to do with politics...He belonged to so many people and each one thought they had him completely and he loved each one...He loved us all... He had each of [them]."[73]

Jackie had them, too; she had her family with the illustrated book of writings and poems she would give as gifts. She had the young man outside the Washington Movie Theater, who lent her and Jack fifteen cents, when she wrote him a thank-you note with three nickels taped to the bottom. She had Charles Whitehouse when she displayed the "courage of a lioness" galloping on horseback across the open fields of Newport. She had Peter, the pool boy at Bailey's Beach, when she picked him up hitchhiking in her black Cadillac and drove him "all the way home" to the "poor Irish" section of Newport. She had the volunteer docent at the JFK Library, whose umbrella shielded her from a driving rain, when, with a genuine gentility of voice, she took his arm and said, "My dear, you are drenched." She had the people of

West Virginia when she kicked off her shoes during one of Jack's campaign speeches in the 1960 primary. She had them all, and there were more—many more—waiting.

She stood beaming at her husband's side in the overcrowded Hyannis Port armory as President-elect John F. Kennedy addressed the nation. "I can assure you that every degree of mind and spirit that I possess," he told them, "will be devoted to the long-range interest of the United States and to the cause of freedom around the world. And now my wife and I prepare for a new administration and a new baby." The new baby arrived sixteen days later, and it was time for Jackie to move again. This time her new address was 1600 Pennsylvania Avenue, Washington, D.C. On January 20, 1961, Jackie, Jack, Caroline and John Fitzgerald Kennedy Jr. moved into the White House, the bearers of the torch for this new generation of Americans. The queen of the circus, who had married the man in the flying trapeze, was on her way to the White House, to be admired by the world's biggies.

## PART II

# The Summer White House

> "All the memories come back, no place in the world as lovely as Hammersmith Farm."
>
> *Jacqueline Kennedy*

Dearest Mummy," wrote Jackie as she prepared to leave Hammersmith Farm on Monday, October 2, 1961. This marked their first visit home to Hammersmith since becoming the first couple of the United States. "You can't imagine what a strange and guilty feeling it is to be sitting on your bed with you coming home tomorrow. You can never guess what this vacation has done for Jack. He said it was the best that he's ever had. The house and the bay are so beautiful, it gives you a lump in the throat even to him who doesn't see it with all the nostalgia that I do."[74]

Jackie's passion for history and mindfulness of her place in it inspired her to create a guest book to be signed by everyone who accompanied Jack on a presidential visit home. That same mindset found Jackie adding a plaque to the desk in Uncle Hughdie's office, where Jack had signed some legislation into law. The plaque lists all the bills that became law at Hammersmith Farm. It was Jackie "who thought of having that plaque made to put on that funny old desk which has always been in this house."[75]

When John F. Kennedy took the oath of office, he stood before his people and his God, declaring to the world, "Let the word go forth from this time and place, to friend and foe alike, that the torch has been passed to a

The staff at Hammersmith Farm await the arrival of Marine I bearing the president and first lady for their first presidential visit. Caroline can be seen standing in front of the chef. Caroline and John often waited on the step for the chopper to land.

new generation of Americans." The Kennedys were the initial first couple to be born in the twentieth century. John Kennedy was the youngest man ever elected president, and at thirty-one, Jackie was the youngest first lady since Woodrow Wilson's daughter served in that capacity in 1915. His predecessor, Dwight Eisenhower, was reelected in 1956 at the age of sixty-six. At the time, he was the oldest man ever elected president, and his wife, Mamie, was sixty-four when they left the White House.

President Kennedy took the unprecedented step of asking a poet to recite at his presidential inauguration. Robert Frost, a fellow New Englander, set that historic precedent. At a press conference surrounding Frost's eighty-fifth birthday, he interjected himself into the upcoming 1960 presidential campaign. Asked about the decline of New England, he responded, "The next President of the United States will be from Boston. Does that sound as if New England is decaying?" Of course the press wanted Frost to name the next president, and he replied, "He's a Puritan named Kennedy. The only

At 3:15 on September 26, 1961, Marine I landed on the front lawn of Hammersmith Farm—a scene that would be re-created many times over the next two years at what came to be known as the Summer White House. Jackie carries Caroline (near the fence) while Jack walks behind.

The first presidential visit to Hammersmith Farm called for a semi-formal family portrait sitting for White House photographer Robert Knudsen. They posed on the same stairwell from which Jackie threw her wedding bouquet in 1953.

Puritans left these days are the Roman Catholics." He added, "There, I guess I wear my politics on my sleeve."[76]

Ten months removed from declaring his intent, Kennedy wrote to Frost, "I just want to send you a note to let you know how gratifying it was to be remembered by you on the occasion of your eighty-fifth birthday. I only regret that the intrusion of my name…took away some of the attention from the man who really deserved it—Robert Frost.[77] In all his subsequent speaking engagements, Frost created the opportunity to openly endorse the Massachusetts junior senator. The presidential hopeful took to ending many campaign speeches with the words from one of Frost's most famous poems: "Stopping by Woods on a Snowy Evening." The popular piece, which Frost penned in about twenty minutes,[78] ends with a call for more work to be done: "The woods are lovely dark and deep. But I have promises to keep. And miles to go before I sleep. And miles to go before I sleep."

When the president-elect invited Frost to participate in his inauguration, he asked if he was planning to recite a new poem. If not, he requested "The Gift Outright," a poem that Frost himself described as "the history of the United States in a dozen [actually sixteen] lines of blank verse."[79] The young president came close to getting both new and old, but a freshly fallen blinding snow and blazing sun eliminated the former. The poet had written, specific for the occasion, a poem he originally called "Dedication," which he planned to read as a preface to the president's requested verse. The glare of the sun reflecting off the snow made it impossible, however, and Frost recited from memory "The Gift Outright." "Dedication," which Frost later changed to "For John F. Kennedy on His Inauguration," ended with:

> The glory of a next Augustan age
> Of a power leading from its strength and pride,
> Of young ambition eager to be tried,
> Firm in our free beliefs without dismay,
> In any game the nations want to play.
> A golden age of poetry and power
> Of which this noonday's the beginning hour.

Before leaving Washington, Frost visited the White House. President and Mrs. Kennedy thanked him, and he presented the president with a manuscript copy of "Dedication," inscribing: "Amended copy. And now let us mend our ways." Frost advised the new president not to let the Harvard in him "get too important." [80] "Poetry and power," wrote Frost, "is the formula for another Augustan Age. Don't be afraid of power." Written on the president's thank-you note were the words, "It's poetry and power all the way!" [81]

The new generation's inclusion of the octogenarian poet served as a clarion call to the "next Augustan age." Poet William Meredith said the inclusion of Frost "focused attention on Kennedy as a man of culture," [82] and *Horizon* magazine's Douglas Cater called Frost's participation the beginning of a "cultural renaissance in America." [83]

As sure as Jack became the face of this "cultural renaissance," it was Jackie who was its designer, architect, and implementer. "The president's curiosity and natural tastes," wrote Arthur Schlesinger, "had been stimulated by Jacqueline's informed and exquisite responses: art had become a normal dimension of existence." [84] The American people were ignited by the passing torch, and Jackie's "informed and exquisite responses" would not be lost on foreign leaders, nor their citizenry. Jackie's impact was immediate and powerful.

"It only took about three weeks after the inauguration," wrote Jackie's social secretary, Tish Baldridge, "for those of us in the White House to realize…we had a huge star on our hands." [85] Jackie received nine thousand letters per week, mostly from women wanting to know everything from her brand of shampoo and lipstick color to how many rollers she put in her hair at night and what baby food she fed little John.

In early April the White House announced plans for its first official state visits: Ottawa, Canada, in mid-May to be followed by a visit to Paris and Charles de Gaulle. There was immediate speculation on behalf of the press that "Mrs. Kennedy…will set a precedent for US First Ladies by acting as the unofficial interpreter between her husband and the French President." [86] Why not? She was a self-proclaimed Francophile, fluent in French, and she carried a BA in French literature from George Washington University. She had lived in France, studying at the Sorbonne, and had read de Gaulle's biography in French. She had also spent some time with him at a garden party in the French Embassy in 1960. "Jack was campaigning in Oregon," Jackie remembered. "I guess I talked to him for about ten minutes...I told him how much Jack admired him."[87] In those ten minutes, she so charmed the French president that upon his departure he said, "The only thing I want to bring back from America is Mrs. Kennedy."

Jackie's charm and elegance captured hearts beyond just de Gaulle's; she also "scored some diplomatic coups with Ambassador and Madame Hervé Alphand."[88] Following the first diplomatic corps reception, Nicole Alphand noted, "You could tell there was a different person there [in the White House] and the lighted candles everywhere...the flowers arranged the way French women do them...natural and a little wild."[89] In France, they wrote of her as if she were a Hollywood starlet: "Her full lips, high cheek bones, widely spaced, heavily lashed eyes, and black hair."[90]

It was April 12, 1961 when worldwide news shouted that the Soviets had successfully launched a man into space. "RUSSIANS PUT MAN IN ORBIT," declared New York's *Daily News*, while in London the *Guardian* announced on its front page, "RUSSIA HAILS COLUMBUS OF SPACE." The Soviets and their cosmonaut, Yuri Gagarin, were the toast of the world. A U.S. setback in both image and prestige, it proved a tiny blip compared to the humiliation awaiting President Kennedy and America in merely five days. The United States launched a CIA-backed and led invasion of Cuba. The campaign's abysmal failure was a crushing blow for the esteem of the United States and its president.

The Bay of Pigs marked the low point in Jack's presidency, and it was the most depressed Jackie ever saw him. "We were down in Glen Ora [Virginia]," Jackie recalled, "with Jean and Steve Smith." At about 5:00 p.m. the president received a phone call from Secretary of State Dean Rusk. "He was sitting on the edge of the bed...and it went on and on and he looked so depressed when it was over." The invasion was underway, and it was clear from the outset that the desired outcome would not be achieved. "Jack just sat there on the bed...looking in pain almost and he went downstairs and you just knew, he knew what had happened was wrong...I just saw him... terribly, really low."[91]

Despite the personal anguish that beset the president and the world's lambasting of the United States, Jack's approval rating rose to 83 percent, the high-water mark of his entire presidency. This was due, in part, to the press conference in which he stated, "Victory has one hundred fathers and defeat is an orphan," and added, "I'm not looking to conceal responsibility, I am the responsible officer of the government." It was in this atmosphere that Jack and Jackie planned their first international excursion, and in mid-May America learned: "Kennedy, Khrush Meet in Vienna June 3, 4."[92]

Speculation about the political ramifications of the meetings with de Gaulle and Khrushchev filled newspapers around the globe. Of no less interest was Jackie and the role she would play. As their departure drew near, the attention intensified. "Paris fashion houses are buzzing with orders from prominent women, all ordering gowns for the receptions to be held during the Kennedys' visit."[93] Interest ran high over what Jackie might wear, what couturiers she might or might not visit, and what shops and other Parisian "delights" she might wish to indulge in. Her role as translator never came to fruition, as her focus became other official goodwill duties. These duties proved far more impactful and ignited a worldwide fascination with the young American president and his thirty-one-year-old first lady.

Jackie threw herself into preparing to execute those duties, which included hiring a tutor to freshen up her French and poring over State Department briefings. Meetings with designer Oleg Cassini organized a wardrobe to please the most critical Parisian eye. "She didn't plan to outshine the president," noted Defense Secretary Robert McNamara, "but she certainly gave thought to what her impact would be and how to plan her behavior and actions in a way that was supportive and compatible." [94]

Canada was the first stop, and as Jackie's staff prepared, they received a visit from Canadian ambassador Arnold Heeney. He met with Tish Baldridge to deliver a preemptive caveat, preparing all for a cool reception from the Canadian people. It would not come from a lack of respect or even affection, but Canadians were just not as demonstrative as Americans. "In fact," he added abjectly, "even the Queen [Elizabeth] is always prepared, but a trifle upset by, the cool reception she receives in Ottawa." [95]

On May 16, the president and first lady were welcomed by 100,000 cheering Ottawans. The city not known for its over-enthusiastic welcomes of state visitors welcomed them enthusiastically, and they loved Jackie. The Canadian press showered her with adulation: "She's a living doll…radiant…a Madonna in an Oleg Cassini outfit" and a "modern day Venus DiMilo." [96]

An hour-long motorcade to the Government House was followed by a greeting by Prime Minister and Mrs. Diefenbaker and the Governor-General and Mrs. Vanier. President and Mrs. Kennedy then partook in the Canadian tradition of tree planting by distinguished visitors. Using silver spade shovels, they turned the soil. "Mr. Kennedy…accepted the shovel…and dug in…his hefty shovels of earth spread around the base of the tree." After four or five shovelfuls he turned to the prime minister and, grinning, said, "Isn't this supposed to be symbolic?" [97] He handed a beaming Diefenbaker the shovel and said, "How about you?" Jackie, on the other hand "had a more feminine approach…her high heels digging into the soft wet grass…she managed a few tiny shovelfuls of earth." [98] Unbeknownst to anyone, Jack had tweaked his famous bad back and then shoveled through the stabbing pain. For the next couple of weeks, he would be using crutches away from the public eye, and on the subsequent trip to Europe he sought refuge as often as possible in a hot bath.

Excited, animated crowds followed Jackie's visit to Canada's National Art Gallery and the exhibition of the "Musical Ride" by the Royal Canadian Mounted Police. They appreciated her genuine enthusiasm in exploring the museum and the fervor with which she applauded the difficult equestrian maneuvers of the Mountys, all prompting one UPI reporter to note, "The American First Lady's only problem was how to cope with adulation." [99] Words like *radiant*, *conquest*, *triumph*, and *smashing* appeared in newspapers throughout the world, describing the reception Jackie received from her northern neighbors. The head of the Canadian senate, Mark Drouin, added, "She has conquered all of our hearts,"[100] while virtually every member in Parliament was in agreement that America's first couple was received with more warmth and enthusiasm than Queen Elizabeth herself. Jackie remembered, "Everyone was saying Ottawa was so cold and never gave receptions...nice ones to anyone." They were "terribly enthusiastic crowds and everyone was flabbergasted." [101]

Tish Baldridge recalled, "The Canadians...screaming Jackie, Jackie in the streets, and Canadians just don't scream like that normally." Following this visit, Jack saw his wife with "new eyes." Somewhat annoyed with the "extra stuff" Jackie packed, "he was very proud of her and of the lavish descriptions of her personal appearance." This brought him to a new understanding; "he realized it was all a very important part of her image of impeccable grooming and beauty and style." [102] It was evident that Jackie invoked as much enthusiasm from the crowd as did Jack. This elicited playful ribbing, which he took with both amusement and pride.

On May 5, Navy Commander Alan B. Shepard became the first American in space, successfully completing a fifteen-minute suborbital flight. The success of the mission lifted the spirits of the nation and took some of the sting out of the Gagarin flight. Days before departing for Europe, President Kennedy lifted the eyes of the nation toward the stars. Speaking before a joint session of Congress, he linked the exploration of space to the worldwide struggle between freedom and tyranny. Realizing the "impact of this adventure [space] on the minds of men everywhere," he set forth a national goal: "I believe this nation should commit itself to achieving the goal, before this decade is out, of landing a man on the moon and returning him safely to the earth."[103]

The world watched and waited to see how the young president, armed with his vision, would fare in his meetings with the seventy-year-old French president and the sixty-seven-year-old Soviet premier.

Jack and Jackie met at New York's Idlewild Airport at 10:00 p.m. on May 30 for the overnight flight to Paris. Their plane landed at 10:30 a.m. the following day. While they were in flight, the citizens of France watched a thirty-minute television interview with President and Mrs. Kennedy. Completed at the White House two weeks earlier, French TV anchor Pierre Crenesse had conducted Jackie's entire interview in French, leaving "Paree wackee, waiting for Jackie."[104] The vast majority of France's two million television sets were tuned in, and anticipation was heightened when she said, "I cannot describe to you my emotions at the thought of again seeing France where I was a student and where I will now be on a state visit with my husband."[105]

President de Gaulle greeted "my dear President" and the asset "at your side...the most gracious, Mrs. Kennedy."[106] He acknowledged the challenges these allies faced, and then President Kennedy spoke. Referring to France as "our oldest friend," Jack touched on the common goals of preserving both freedom and peace. A forty-five-minute motorcade followed through the streets of Paris, to the Quai d'Orsai, the French government's guest palace, where Tish Baldridge was waiting. "I stood on the balcony...and watched the procession." The "marvelous *Garde Republicaine* [French Honor Guard] on the horses and those wonderful steel helmets glittering in the sunshine, their long plumes waving behind and the clipclop of the horses' hooves and the marvelous blaring of the trumpets. And then to see the French, the blasé French, erupting with joy and surprise as this handsome young couple appeared!"[107]

With ardent fervor, one and a half million Parisians greeted President Kennedy with shouts of "Viva Kennedy!" as he rode, with President de Gaulle, in the motorcade's lead car. Jackie followed with Madame de Gaulle, and she was met with unbridled enthusiasm as cries of "Jacqu-ie, Jacqu-ie!" and "Viva Jacqu-leen!" rose from the crowd. "People fainted in the crush," Baldridge remembered, "and the sounds of ambulance sirens mingled with the roar of fighter jets...overhead...The noise was deafening...The cries of Viva l'Amerique rang out from tongues that spoke many languages. And through it all, the constant chant Jacqu-ie, Jacqu-ie".[108]

"She drew a larger crowd than he did," said Baldridge, "and he laughed about it," while chiding that "he should be jealous." Jack could not contain his joy at the reception Jackie received. "The president was so very, very proud of her," Baldridge recalled, "and the marvelous way she handled herself."[109] As much as they admired the American president, their affinity for Jackie went a little further and was best articulated by a Parisian cabbie. "We respect the president for all his actions and his courage," he said, but alluding to Jackie's French ancestry, it came down to one simple fact: "Madame, after all, is French."[110] It was clear "from the moment of her smiling arrival...the radiant young first lady was the Kennedy who really mattered."[111]

Within an hour Jack left for a forty-minute private meeting with de Gaulle. Jackie and the presidential entourage joined them for luncheon. Built in 1722, the Elysee palace was home to General de Gaulle for the ten years he served as president. Jackie was seated next to de Gaulle. Having already impressed him a year ago, Jackie now enchanted him, asking him "things of history...all the things I wanted to know...like who did Louis XVI's daughter marry...did she have any children?" At one point de Gaulle "leaned across the table to Jack...and said in French, 'Mrs. Kennedy knows more French history than most Frenchwomen.'"[112] *Time* magazine reported that "Jacqueline zeroed in with a flashing smile and began to speak in her low slow French. The glacial Charles de Gaulle promptly melted."[113]

Sitting across from McGeorge Bundy, the seventy-year-old general and now president, who had led the French resistance against the Nazis in World War II and then headed the provisional government reestablishing France's democracy, learned firsthand that the torch had been passed to a new generation of Americans. "You know, Bundy looks very young," Jackie said, recalling the event, "and de Gaulle asked who he was." "Head of National Security," she replied, then added, "The most brilliant young head at Harvard." In his characteristic pompous air, de Gaulle asked Bundy a question in a condescendingly "slow French," and Bundy shot back his answer in clear, articulate French. "I was so proud," said Jackie. "First run for our side."[114]

Seasoned diplomat Charles Bohlen observed, "There's a tremendous value in Mrs. Kennedy's fluent French and charming youthfulness." Jackie's company buoyed the spirits of the French president putting him "visibly in a very good mood."[115] This was not a condition often observed.

Following lunch, Jackie visited a children's medical clinic that was started by the American Red Cross following World War I. A crowd of nearly two thousand gathered quickly to catch a glimpse of the first lady. Comprised primarily of mothers with children in their arms, they patiently waited while Jackie toured the facility. Exiting, she addressed the gathering in French, telling them she would send furniture to outfit the clinic's reception area. As she entered her car, about one thousand people broke through police barriers. Streaming across the street shouting "Bravo!" and "Viva Jackie!" they swarmed around her vehicle, peering through the windows and gushing compliments. Jackie sat smiling, composed, repeating over and over again, "Merci, merci."[116] It was just more of the "blasé French erupting with joy."

The crème de la crème for Jackie came on the eve of departure, when President and Madame de Gaulle hosted dinner at the Palace of Versailles.

For Baldridge it invoked memories of when she and Jackie had toured the palace. As schoolgirls the pair would dream about what it would be like to live as a member of the court of Louis XIV, and now at that very same palace Jackie was a guest of honor.

Dinner took place in the Hall of Mirrors around a long rectangular table adorned with exquisite porcelain, elegant crystal, and splendid silver. An eighteenth-century candelabra held flickering candles that cast a mystical glow on the refurbished frescoes looking down from the ceiling.

Following a six-course dinner accompanied by three wines and champagne, the après dinner entertainment provided a stroll back in time to the court of French royalty of which Jackie had dreamed as a child. Musicians, dressed in eighteenth-century costumes, appeared through the darkened corridors playing period instruments. Led by liveried footmen bearing burning candelabras, the presidential entourage wound their way through long, darkened hallways to the palace theater. "There seated on tiny chairs fit for eighteenth century legs and posteriors…we watched a ballet commissioned for Louis XV, with torches as spotlights, performed just as it would have been for the king." [117] Wrapped in the splendor and majesty of a childhood fantasy, Jackie was beside herself with joy. "I thought I was in heaven," she said. "I have never seen anything like it." [118]

The allure of the evening continued as they motored back to the Quai d'Orsai. Weaving its way through the magical gardens of Versailles, the lead car bearing Jackie and Jack stopped as it came upon an illuminated fountain. They emerged and walked toward the fountain. Reaching its edge, they paused, watching as diamond sprays leaped into the darkened sky, twinkling when captured by the light. There they stood, hand and hand, sharing a moment that belonged to them and only them: the first lady of the United States and her president.

The following day, their last in Paris, the president held a press conference. In his opening statement he encapsulated the impact Jackie had on the state visit. "I do not think it, altogether inappropriate," he said, "to introduce myself to this audience. I am the man who accompanied Jacqueline Kennedy to Paris. And I have enjoyed it." Longtime diplomat David Bruce added, "Jackie proved herself more valuable to United States prestige than ten divisions."[119]

Khrushchev was already in Vienna, and within twenty minutes of the first couple's arrival, Jack was in a meeting with the Soviet premier. Following the meeting came a luncheon at the American Embassy and dinner at the Schoenbrunn Palace. Built in 1642 and remodeled in 1740, it served as home to emperors and as Allied headquarters during World War II. With the reestablishment of the Austrian Republic, it became a museum open for special events. Bringing together the two most powerful men in the world certainly qualified as a special event.

Described by Jack as a "combination of external jocosity and internal rage,"[120] Khrushchev had a reputation for both public and private belligerence. Jack experienced it privately, and in his most celebrated public display, Khrushchev removed his shoe at the United Nations, waved it, and then banged it on his rostrum while nearly coming to blows with Filipino delegate Lorenzo Sumulong.

At dinner, it did not take Jackie long to cut through the gruff exterior of the bombastic premier. "Jack had advised me to stay away from political talk...talk to them about something different...I'd just read *The Sabres of Paradise* by Lesley Blanch," she recalled, "which was all about the Ukraine in the nineteenth century and the wars and things...It sounded to me so rather romantic. I was telling him how I loved all that and the dance, the lezginka and the Kabarda stallion." Khrushchev responded with a quick rundown of how the government had placed more teachers in the Ukraine, and they were now producing more wheat. "Oh, Mr. Chairman President," came Jackie's slightly admonishing reply, "Don't bore me with that, I think the romantic is so much [better]." The chairman responded with a hearty laugh, and it became clear to Jackie that "at last, he could let down too." From then on it was "just one gag after another…like sitting next to Abbott and Costello[121] or something."

Jackie found the Soviet women tougher to engage. De Gaulle cautioned her about Madame Khrushchev. "Mefiez vous, c'est elle la plus maline," he told her. ("Watch out, it's she who is the craftier of the two.") Jackie found her and Mrs. Dobrynin (the wife of the head of the foreign ministry) to be somewhat patronizing and condescending. "Both of them have this really gamesmanship thing," Jackie recalled. "If you'd smoke they'd say 'Russian women don't smoke.'" They asked, "Did you go to engineering school?" Their inquiries were designed towards "trying to make themselves seem better…I suppose it was a chip on their shoulder," Jackie concluded. Ever the refined debutante, she fought the uncomfortable air and continued "trying to be polite." Reflecting on the Soviet first lady, Jackie concurred with de Gaulle. "Yeah, she was a bit maline [crafty]…I got sick of…those little digs all the time."[122]

However, Jackie sensed a deep shyness in the difficult woman and twice reached out to compassionately guide her through it. The first time came at lunch, where Jackie was rendezvousing with Madame Khrushchev at the Palais Pallavicini. Crowds had gathered in the Platz awaiting their separate arrivals. Mrs. Khrushchev was first on the scene and was greeted with respectful, warm applause. "When Mrs. Kennedy's car appeared…a ripple of excitement ran down the packed lines," and "the gentle policeman… restrained the enthusiasts." The delighted Viennese chanted, "Jackie, Jackie!" as she smiled and waved to the crowd. When she disappeared inside, a collective moan of disappointment rose from the gatherers, and immediately the chant resumed, "Jackie, Jackie, Jackie!"[123] Jackie walked over to the open window and waved. "The crowd erupted and the noise was terrific." Turning away from the window, and cognizant that there were no voices calling for Madame Khrushchev, Jackie went to the Soviet first lady. "They want to see you too," she said, leading her to the open window.[124] "A familiar shining dark head appeared and inches below a curly grey one... It was Jackie and Nnia [*sic*] side by side...Jackie smiled her smile and Mrs. Khrushchev beamed. The crowd cheered."[125]

Dinner at the palace was made uncomfortable for Jackie by a conflict of protocols: the international protocol of heads of state and Jackie's personal protocol. "I outranked her," Jackie explained, "because Jack was president and Khrushchev was just chairman...so she wouldn't leave the room before I did. I didn't like to go before an older woman...and...she was just hanging back." A stalemate ensued until Jackie acted. "I took her by the hand and said, well I'm very shy and so you have to come with me," and the two left the room hand in hand. Thrilled at Jackie's solution to their dilemma, the Soviet first lady darted over to a Russian in her party. "Did you hear what she said to me?" she exclaimed, "sort of beaming." This caused Jackie to conclude of the Soviets that they "have their little chips," but "they're all shy underneath."[126]

On December 1, 1963, a mere six days after Jack's funeral, Jackie wrote a letter to Khrushchev. It read, in part:

> *Dear Mr. Chairman President,*
> *You and he were adversaries, but you were allied in a determination that the world should not be blown up. You respected each other and could deal with each other... The danger that troubled my husband was that war might not be started so much by the big men but by the little ones. While big men know the needs for self-control and restraint, little men are sometimes moved by fear and pride. If only in the future the big men can make the little ones sit down and talk, before they fight..."*

Citing their meeting in Vienna, she concluded,

> *"I read that [your wife] had tears in her eyes when she left the American Embassy in Moscow, after she signed the mourning book. Please thank her for that.*
>
> *Sincerely, Jacqueline Kennedy."* [127]

The trip ended with an overnight stay in London, where crowds chanting, "We want Jack and we want Jackie!" broke through barriers outside Buckingham Palace as they dined with the queen. Coupling a state visit with the christening of their niece Anna Christina at Westminster Cathedral, they stayed at the home of Jackie's sister Lee and Stas Radziwill. "Mrs. Kennedy... won princess like acclaim in London, as quickly as she had triumphed earlier over Paris and Vienna." [128] Jackie remained in London when Jack went home and then spent a week traveling with Stas and Lee.

The thirty-one-year-old first lady enraptured de Gaulle, beguiled Khrushchev, charmed Madame de Gaulle, and protected Madame Khrushchev—an astonishing performance when one considers that she was not even half the age of the pair of crusty, seasoned European leaders and their respective first ladies. Hundreds of newspapers from Boston to Honolulu, Racine to Brownsville, and all stops in between smothered their front pages extolling the virtues of Jackie and her remarkable European exploits.

Using myriad phrases under a multitude of headlines, copy editors nationwide sought to capture Jackie's impact: "Le coup de foudre, love at first sight," said one under its heading, "Paris Falls in Love with Jacqueline." [129] Boston declared, "Head Over Their French Heels, Paris Falls for Jacqueline," adding, "Jacqueline Kennedy and France were made for each other." [130] Tampa proclaimed, "La Tres Belle [the very beautiful] Jackie...Mrs. Kennedy Charms French." [131] And Texas touted, "Jackie Turns Scene Stealer." [132]

The effusive praise emanated from Vienna, as well. A Baltimore headline included an "Often-Grim Nikita" as a "Jacqueline Triumph." "A twinkle lit his eye" as he was "shifting his chair closer" to share the musical part of the evening next to her.[133] The west Texas town of El Paso announced, "Krushy Twinkles at Jackie,"[134] while the *Oklahoman* splashed a huge front-page photo of Krushy, "a twinkle in his eyes" fervently gazing at a smiling Jackie.[135] Racine trumpeted, "Jacqueline Wows Nikita," referring to Jackie's "elegant triumph" and noting, "The tough and often belligerent Communist leader looked like a smitten schoolboy."[136]

Jackie had become an international superstar. "The Jackie Look," now a regular selling point on New York's Seventh Avenue, went worldwide. The Polish magazine *Swait* wrote, "The face and silhouette of Jackie are known to all people all over the civilized world."[137] She even penetrated the Iron Curtain, where a Leningrad fashion magazine advertised "Jackie Look" clothes. "The deck has shifted,"[138] Protocol Officer Angier Biddle Duke told his soon-to-be-wife, Robin. Jackie had replaced Jack as the face of the administration.

She had become, in a sense, a roving ambassador for her husband. Tish Baldridge recalled her emergence as an international force. Not enamored with the backroom politicking and arm twisting necessary in garnering votes, Jackie nevertheless was "such a bright, intelligent person...interested in the issues. She very definitely shared his opinions and interrogated him as to what was going on...and she helped him. She would write hand-written letters and go on for pages and pages to General de Gaulle and Prime Minister Nehru and all...this was her way to further the political gains of the United States of America and its foreign policy. I am sure no other First Lady has ever done that."[139] Lyndon Johnson witnessed her allure firsthand in Texas when she delivered a speech in Spanish the night before Jack died. So impressed was he that, in 1964, he openly spoke of offering her the position of Mexican ambassador.

Inspired by Vienna, London, and above all, Versailles, Jackie returned and began preparing to welcome Pakistan's president Ayub Khan in a way that no foreign leader had ever been welcomed to the United States.

Jackie joined Jack on Marine I to welcome Pakistani president Ayub Khan to Newport as their extended Hammersmith stay was drawing to a close. Here she greets Khan with a handshake. On the right is Angier Biddle Duke, the U.S. chief of protocol.

In the early days of the administration, Tish Baldridge received a phone call from Cecil Wall, the director of Mount Vernon. Suggesting "a little special entertaining for special pals,"[140] he extended an invitation to the White House, offering Washington's Potomac River estate for use any evening throughout the summer. Baldridge crafted a memo to Mrs. Kennedy stating the same, never guessing that "a little special entertaining for special pals" would turn into the most historic state dinner in American history.

The "special pal" was Pakistan's president Mohammad Ayub Khan. Khan came to power in 1958 as a result of a military coup. He endeared himself to America and the Kennedy administration with his general anti-communist stance and his commitment of five thousand of his finest troops to battle communist forces in Laos. "Anything Ayub wants from me now," the

They returned to Hammersmith for lunch, and then Khan went on to Washington where they met him for evening festivities. Jackie and Khan went riding the next day in Virginia. This was their third official meeting; the state dinner at Mount Vernon and Jackie's trip to Pakistan in March of 1962 marked the first two.

president told Kenny O'Donnell, "he can have."[141] What he got, for starters, came compliments of Jackie.

Jackie was basking in a whole new light, having learned to "use power with tact and reticence," leaving "all the men…in love with [her]."[142] Her influence was not lost on the diplomatic corps or foreign heads of state. De Gaulle himself adroitly observed Jackie's augmentation to the

Kennedy presidency "without mixing in politics…she played the game very intelligently." [143] Kenneth Galbraith, Indian ambassador, offered the most compelling synopsis: Jackie "would observe, hear, and render judgment… She distinguished sharply between those who were serving him and those who were serving themselves…especially…the accomplished frauds. Her wise and astringent analysis was especially important to Jack Kennedy." Jackie was fully aware of her place and what she brought to Jack and his presidency. "I was an observer," she wrote to British prime minister Harold Macmillan, "not a participant as [Jack] didn't wish his wife to be that way. He knew I did not miss much…and that I was so aware of all that he was doing. He was proud that I knew." [144] Jack counted on her insight into people, no matter their status or station.

Energized by her experience at Versailles, a veritable tiptoe through the days of Louis XIV, Jackie was intrigued with the prospect of unveiling a piece of America's past. What better vehicle than a state dinner, and what better venue than the home of the man who commanded the army that won America's independence and then presided over its first government? First, however, it would have to be ascertained whether the venue was suitable for such an undertaking. Jackie headed a group of eight, including Baldridge, Cecil Wall, and Francis Beirne, the regent of the Mount Vernon Ladies Association, meeting them on the premises for an escorted tour.

Built on land garnered by George Washington's great-great-grandfather John in 1674, construction began on the current home in 1734, when the future president was two years old. Construction continued throughout four decades, with the final product completed in 1778.

Needless to say, the common, modern niceties were missing or rudimentary at best. Baldridge noted there was "virtually no electricity, no heating, limited restroom and kitchen facilities." [145] It was clear the antiquated home presented far too many obstacles to provide the amenities necessary to host a state dinner. Jackie, on the other hand, was enchanted, which fueled her desire to showcase the home of the father of the country. "One look at Jackie's animated face," recalled Baldridge, "and I knew we were all doomed." [146]

What the staff viewed as unconquerable hurdles, Jackie saw as opportunities, and in her soothing, charming way she pelted Wall and Beirne with questions. She wanted to know how the bathrooms and parking could be accommodated. The dining she had already settled in her mind, and all she needed to know was where on the lawn it was flat enough to put up a beautiful tent.

Francis Beirne was flabbergasted, yet her own sense of history found the idea exciting. It became her burden to bring Mrs. Kennedy's idea back to the Board of Regents, who owned, maintained, and operated Mount Vernon. Initially consternated at the thought of over one hundred people making merry with food and drink on General Washington's front lawn, Mrs. Beirne convinced them of the value of playing host to the dinner, and they approved it. It now fell to Tish Baldridge and her "doomed" staff to execute what was to become one of the most memorable nights of Jack and Jackie's 1,037 days in the White House.

They had just short of a month to pull it off, the same time frame normally used to plan a simple dinner at the White House. There was nothing simple about this affair, however, as virtually "every single item had to be transported to the site." [147] Standing on the lawn Jackie visualized everything from the guests arriving via boats on the Potomac (Jack's idea), to the tent color and the plates, flowers, and vases to be placed at the sixteen circular tables that would seat eight.

The government VIPs would be intermingled, separated from their spouses at different tables—Jack with Khan's daughter, Nasir Aurangzeb, and Jackie with the Pakistani president. No detail was overlooked. Practice runs up and down the Potomac revealed that, despite the daytime temperatures, the evenings were often breezy, bringing a chill upon the river. This was remedied by placing on each boat "a delightful hodge-podge of...sweaters and chiffon scarves…French designer things lent by Jackie and items from Bloomingdales and Macys lent by the rest of us." [148] Nagging summer insects presented a major challenge. In a measure that clearly indicates a bygone era, "the mosquitos and chiggers failed to feast upon the banquetiers [*sic*]… because the area had been thoroughly doused with insecticides well in advance." [149] It was actually a bit more complicated than that, however. The lawn was mowed in the early afternoon and then sprayed to eliminate the critters awakened by the clamor. By 4:00 p.m. "the mosquitos were holding their own state dinner and the sprayers were ordered back to work."[150] The food had just arrived from the White House, and as the insecticide hovered over the lawn, a breeze from the river carried the perilous cloud toward the kitchen tent. White House chef Rene Verdon, worried that the food might have been compromised, openly wondered if the guests would die if they ate it. Two brave Secret Service agents acted as court tasters. Neither of them died, and both reported the food tasted just fine.

Four boats cruised the Potomac for an hour and fifteen minutes listening to the strings of live orchestras. Jack and Khan's daughter, Nasir, hosted on the *Honey Fitz*, while Jackie, President Khan and Speaker of the House Sam Rayburn welcomed guests on the *Sequoia*. As they approached the Mount Vernon Pier they came to a stop across the river. With all the military at attention and saluting, they listened as the national anthem flowed over the trees and across the river, bringing everyone to a halt. "There was not a dry eye on the river," recalled Tish Baldridge. "Even the Pakistanis were undone by that." [151]

Inspired by her stroll through French history at Versailles, Jackie delighted the guests with her own orchestrated, dazzling transport to America's nascent days. Limousines greeted them as they disembarked, carrying them past the Marine honor guards who lined both sides of the winding road to Washington's home. Mint juleps were served in silver cups on the veranda following a tour of the mansion. Washington's recipe for the bourbon libation was followed, while frosted orange drinks were offered to accommodate the Muslim guests who did not imbibe alcohol.

Fifty Marines bearing the colors of each state rimmed the lawn of the circular drive as the Army Color Guard and Fife and Drum Corps performed close-order drills. The guests stood in rapt attention as the unit, bedecked in the scarlet redcoats, powdered wigs, and tri-cornered hats of Washington's Continental Army, performed the drill of their forbears. The drill ended with the firing of blank muskets across the green. The White House Press Corps had assembled there, and through the wafting cloud of white smoke appeared a handkerchief waving the white flag of surrender. President Kennedy roared with laughter. "That's the press corps," he said to his Pakistani counterpart. Khan, also laughing, said, "I'm so glad, that's just what we would have done in our country." [152]

The military display ended, and all moved into the tent for dinner, which began with a toast. President Kennedy honored his guest by likening him to Washington in leading his fledgling country in their struggle for independence. He invoked Washington's words from a letter he wrote to David Stuart[153]. "I had rather be at Mount Vernon with a friend or two about me, than to be attended at the seat of government by the officers of state and the representatives of every power in Europe." [154]

Dusk was melting into darkness as the lights of the Coast Guard boats crisscrossing the Potomac sent sparkles rippling along the surface of the river. The candlelight of the hurricane lamps twinkled off crystal goblets and diamond earrings, reflecting shimmers of light everywhere. A group of fireflies even appeared and hovered over the lawn, creating a mystical glow. The Strolling Strings of the U.S. Air Force meandered among the tables, their violins singing with romantic ballads, and presiding over it all was Jackie—smiling, shining, radiant.

On a makeshift stage, with floodlights silhouetting clusters of trees, some of which Washington actually planted, the seventy-four-piece National

Symphony Orchestra brought the evening to a splendid close. The guests sipped champagne to the strains of Mozart, Debussy, Martin Gould, and George Gershwin. Liszts' "Rakoczy March" brought the magical night to an end and President Kennedy to his feet. "The history making White House social venture, conceived by Mr. Kennedy's wife Jacqueline...went off without a hitch."[155]

Jackie had unveiled a piece of America's past with the same elegance, grace and style that had been unveiled at the Palace of Versailles a few short weeks earlier.

Locals gathered around St. Mary's every time Jack and Jackie were in Newport, waiting and hoping to get a glimpse of the first couple coming to church or leaving.

Two months later, Jack and Jackie made their first presidential visit to Hammersmith Farm, arriving on Tuesday, September 26, following the president's UN speech the day before. On Wednesday, at the Newport War College, the president introduced John McCone as the new director designate of the CIA, replacing Allen Dulles. Then it was back to Hammersmith Farm, the *Honey Fitz* and sitting by the bay.

On Thursday morning, Clint Hill, the agent charged with Mrs. Kennedy's protection, received a call at the Secret Service Command Post. "Mr. Hill," Jackie said, "I was hoping to go out water skiing this afternoon. Will you make sure you have my skis on the jet boat?" A veteran of two previous presidents, Hill was taken aback. "Water skiing?" he repeated. "Are you sure? Do you realize how cold the water is, Mrs. Kennedy?"

"That doesn't bother me," came her amused reply. "I've got a skin diving suit. I'll be fine." The cavalier, matter-of-fact response elicited a chuckle from Hill.

"Mrs. Kennedy," he said, "I hope you realize that the press will be dying to get a picture of you in that wet suit…I can tell you Mamie Eisenhower and Bess Truman never went water skiing, with or without a wet suit."

Laughing, she responded, "Well, now you know I have to go, Mr. Hill."[156]

Returning from her ocean excursion, Jackie hitched a buggy up to Caroline's pony, Macaroni, and ushered Caroline and her baby brother down Harrison Avenue. Mornings and evenings found them relaxing on Narragansett Bay. "We sit for hours on the terrace, just looking at the bay and drinking in the beauty," she wrote, "and all one's strength is renewed." [157] It was the first time since he had assumed the presidency that Jack actually relaxed.

The first presidential visit to the homestead was dedicated primarily to relaxation, which meant, time to be on and by the sea. A plane from Washington arrived every day, dumping a pouch of papers and intelligence briefings, and Jack had access to the White House by virtue of a special phone

In between races, time was spent sailing the Coast Guard yacht *Manitou*. In the top photo, Jackie shares a moment with Fiat heir Gianni Agnelli. In the bottom shot, "Mummy" is cooling off some chowder, while sister Janet is at the tiller. Brother "Yusha" is in red. On the left is former Secretary of State John Kerry, who was dating Janet at the time, and to his left Nina Auchincloss.

hookup. However, he took few calls and reread an old favorite book of his: *Talleyrand* by Alfred Duff Cooper.[158]

Following another water skiing adventure on Friday, Jackie was off to Newport Country Club for a little golf. Accompanied by Clint Hill and longtime friend William Walton, Jackie looked like a natural as, Hill observed, "she hit the ball long and straight...With almost any sport she tried, she was a natural...she was determined to do well."[159]

Jackie was often maligned as too soft or dainty to engage with the rough-and-tumble Kennedy clan; however, she was an outstanding athlete in her own right. An award-winning, highly accomplished equestrian from the age of three, a water skier, and an adept tennis player, her competitive nature was perhaps best revealed through golf.

She had just taken up golf in earnest with lessons from Hyannis club pro Tom Niblet. "Tom, you have your work cut out for you," she told him in their initial meeting. However, her athleticism was apparent in her body movement. She was "very well coordinated," said Niblet, and she moved with an "athletic grace." Her competitive nature was revealed when Niblet inquired what her objectives were regarding the game. She fired back quickly, "To beat my sisters-in-law."[160] She improved rapidly, but she was never willing to substitute her time riding for time on the golf course.

At 3:30 p.m. on Monday Jack rode the *Honey Fitz* to the dock at Quonset Navy Base to board

The Bradlees accompanied Jack and Jackie to celebrate with them their tenth wedding anniversary in Newport. Part of the celebration included some golf at the Newport Country Club where Jackie tees off.

Air Force I for his return to Washington. Jackie went home and, in the quiet of the Hammersmith evening, wrote to her mother: "You can't imagine what you have done for the country by letting us come here, for Jack to have a rest. He was much tireder [*sic*] than I ever thought and now he is ready to start again."[161]

The escape served as a boon to Jack's outlook, demeanor, and energy. "He's like he used to be," Jackie wrote, "laughing and full of jokes...not preoccupied or exhausted the way he has been." His elevated spirit was not lost on those around him. "Charlie Bartlett and Bill Walton couldn't get over it." And at the White House, "everyone was saying what a great mood the prez was in after his vacation."[162]

The family signed the guestbook before departure. Caroline drew a picture of the pond and dictated to her mother, who wrote, "I like the pond I got wet in," while little John added his first scribbles to the occasion. Thinking ahead, Jack added the notation, "What about next year?" and Jackie dittoed his marks, closing with: "All the memories come back, no place in the world as lovely as Hammersmith Farm."[163]

In November they returned to receive Indian prime minister Jawaharlal Nehru, Hammersmith Farm's first head of state. Leaving Hyannis Port, Jack, Jackie, and Caroline, accompanied by Lem Billings and General Clifton, arrived via the forty-minute helicopter ride, and within fifteen minutes they were aboard the *Honey Fitz* on Narragansett Bay.

It was just before noon on Monday, November 6, 1961, when President Kennedy and Indian ambassador John Kenneth Galbraith greeted Nehru and his daughter, Indira Gandhi, at Quonset Naval Base. Jackie, who was scheduled to visit both India and Pakistan at the end of the month, was awaiting them at Hammersmith.

The president and prime minister shook hands warmly before boarding the *Honey Fitz* for the ten-minute cruise to Hammersmith Farm. Along the way, the president pointed out a few of the majestic estates on the bay and, exhibiting his classic wit, said to the seventy-one-year-old prime minister, "I wanted you to see the way the average American family lives." [164] Not particularly tickled, Nehru informed the president that he'd been informed of American affluence. Jackie, with Caroline in hand, greeted the prime minister when they reached the farm. "She'd picked a little flower for him and made a curtsey," Jackie recalled. "That's the first time he sort of smiled." [165]

In what Jackie described as "damned spoiled brattishness," a drink was shared before lunch, during which time Nehru "never said a word... It was just such heavy going." [166] The pre-lunch cocktail lasted just under fifteen minutes, and then Nehru joined the president and aides in the dining room. Jackie dined with Indira Gandhi and Lem Billings in the living room. The short preliminary was not enough time for Jackie to crack the icy "brattishness" of the prime minister, a task she had executed flawlessly with Nikita Khrushchev.

Jack also watched Nehru fall into virtual silence when discussion turned to Vietnam. In the living room, Billings and Jackie found Madam Gandhi "really quite amusing." Displaying a self-deprecating sense of humor, she related stories "about the growing up years and her relationship to her father." She spoke of her political experiences in India and her early struggles, "not only in public speaking, but in accomplishing things not expected of women at that time." The two came away having "enjoyed her immensely."[167]

As the day progressed a different impression of Madame Gandhi emerged. She was irked that she did not dine with the men. "She hated that," recalled Jackie. "She liked to be with the men."[168] Chilliness carried onto Marine I from Hammersmith to Quonset and continued on the ride to Washington. "The president flicked through newspapers...Nehru read *National Geographic*, Indira looked at *Vogue* and Jackie was immersed in Malraux."[169] At the White House dinner Gandhi admonished the president about American policy and sang the praises of a staunch anti-American in

New Delhi. "She is a real prune, bitter, kind of a pushy horrible woman," opined Jackie. "I just don't like her a bit. It always looks like she's been sucking on a lemon."[170] However, Nehru sat between Jackie and Lee, and the charm of the Bouvier sisters lit the "light of love" in Nehru's eyes, thawing the icy premier. By evening's end Jackie knew she was not prepared to visit India two weeks hence, and the trip was rescheduled for the spring.

The thaw did bring some light-hearted banter to the remainder of the week, as Jackie informed Jack how Billings and Madame Gandhi had hit it off at lunch. The Indian contingent was staying at the Blair House, from which Billings began receiving phone calls. "On Sunday afternoon, I received many phone calls, presumably from Madame Gandhi." The calls continued throughout the evening, expressing "her desire to see me, to have dinner with me." Each time Billings returned the call, Madame Gandhi was either out or unavailable. It took some time before Lem realized that the "whole thing was a hoax arranged through the White House switchboard."[171]

Before Nehru left Washington, Jackie found him "easy and charming."[172] However, not so his daughter. "One of those women who when marriage and love and all of those things don't turn out right...It all goes back inside you and the poison works inside like an ulcer...She's a truly bitter woman."[173]

In March 1962, more than 100,000 people lined the streets welcoming Jackie and Lee to India. In preparation, Jackie read Nehru's autobiography, which served as a catalyst for conversation. Jackie came to know Nehru. "He was terribly sweet to Lee and I...He would come home every afternoon and take us for walks in the garden and we'd feed the Pandas. He used to walk me back to my bedroom...and sit in there for about an hour and talk to me...I asked him about the times in prison and everything...his life." Nehru's youngest sister, Krisna Nehru Hutheesing, would also visit with them. "It's so good for my brother to have you two girls here," she told them. "It's some relaxation....His daughter fills the poor man's life with politics. It's politics at lunch, politics at tea, politics at dinner. He never has any relaxation."[174]

Jackie concluded that her trip to India was "a relaxation for him, the kind of thing I'd try to bring into Jack's life in our evenings at home. Someone who wasn't connected to what was worrying him all day."[175] Jackie did for Nehru what she did for Jack: she created a place to rest, a place to relax, a place that was not "connected to what he was worrying about all day."

It was May before she saw Newport again. Traveling first to Groton, Connecticut, along with her mom, she christened the USS *Lafayette*, a nuclear-powered Polaris sub. Outside the gates of the naval base was a small gathering of pacifists protesting this addition to the fleet. Jackie earned a protester's caveat, for among the crowd was a sign that read, "Jackie si, Polaris no."[176] A luncheon followed, and then Jackie and Janet were bound for Hammersmith to work out the details of a planned presidential vacation in September.

In late September 1961 Jackie and Jack enjoyed their "best vacation" of the summer, as Hammersmith and Newport provided far more privacy and space than Hyannis Port. Seeking more of both, in 1962 they rented a home on Squaw Island, around the corner and away from the Kennedy compound.

The following day, Jackie, Janet, and a local attorney viewed four homes in the vicinity of Hammersmith Farm with an eye toward renting one in August and September. Reports circulated that they would lease one on Ruggles Avenue, but these were quickly squashed in a White House statement. "Mrs. Kennedy has not leased any house in Newport and really doesn't know what her summer plans are."[177] Hammersmith Farm would more than suffice as the summer White House for September's America's Cup races.

As for August, Jackie and Caroline were bound for Italy. Leaving John at Hammersmith with Gran Mere Janet, the girls rendezvoused with Lee, her husband Prince Radziwill, and their son Tony for three weeks on Italy's Mediterranean coast. The Villa Episcopio, a 900-year-old ancient palace of

Caroline feeds her pony Macaroni. A gift from Vice President Lyndon B. Johnson, Macaroni was well traveled, spending summers in Newport, autumns in Virginia, and winters at the White House.

The Bailey's Beach pool was a frequent stop with the kids. Here, Jack is in the water helping John muster up the courage to take the leap.

Ravello bishops, carved into the rocky cliffs overlooking the breathtaking Amalfi Coast, served as their home abroad.

While Caroline and "America's first lady," clad in a "pea green one piece bathing suit…splashed merrily in knee deep water of the blue Mediterranean,"[178] Hammersmith Farm served as the "banner attraction" of the third annual mansion tour of the Newport County Preservation Society. Nearly 3,500 patrons, curious for a look into the private world of the president and first lady, filed through the summer White House. Early arrivals caught a glimpse of young John, but later visitors settled for a walk through the stables where the children often played.

Air Force I touched down at Quonset at 6:55 p.m. on August 31, 1962. Jack, Bobby, and Ethel were on board, and Jackie and Caroline were due within the hour. The commensurate welcoming took place: a twenty-one-gun salute, a band, a welcome from Governor Notte, hundreds of Navy men in dress whites, and about a thousand onlookers. True to form, Jack made his way through the crowd accepting well wishes and shaking hands.

Within a half hour, the Caroline touched down, taxiing nose to nose with Air Force I, as the band played the national anthem. Jack boarded the plane alone and within two minutes reappeared with Caroline in hand and Jackie following them down the ramp. After a brief conversation with the governor and naval officers, it was off on Marine I for the hop across Narragansett Bay to Hammersmith's lawn, where John awaited them.

The *Newport Daily News* welcomed the president with an editorial expressing the hope that he could "suspend the cares of his important office not for a mere weekend but a succession of stays from the White House."[179] The succession of days turned into the better part of four weeks, and although the cares could never be completely suspended, there were luncheons on the *Honey Fitz*, sailing on the *Manitou*, and swimming in the heated pool of Mrs. Robert Young on Ruggles Avenue or the one at Bailey's Beach.

Jackie and Jack arrive at the Breakers for a dinner hosted by the Australian Ambassador and Lady Beale (in orange on left). It was the night before the first 1962 America's Cup races. Jack delivered a famous speech about humans' connection to the sea. The ambassador called him first rate.

Jack and Jackie share a moment with Australian Ambassador Sir Howard Beale at the Breakers the night before the America's Cup challenge in September 1962. Beale said of Jackie, "I fell in love with her. She was great company, bubbly and just nicely irreverent."

Jackie observes the fourth America's Cup race from the top deck of the USS *Kennedy* in late September 1962.

Jackie shares a moment with Rhode Island senator Claiborne Pell (left) and Jack's Naval aide Tazewell Shepard on the deck of the *Kennedy* during the fourth race of the America's Cup. It was Pell who sponsored the bill that named the National Center for the Arts the John F. Kennedy Center for the Performing Arts.

Jackie relaxes on the deck of the USS *Joseph P Kennedy Jr.*, during a break in the action of the first race of the America's Cup. She is conversing with Franklin Roosevelt Jr. (standing, white shirt) while Jack converses with Pierre Salinger.

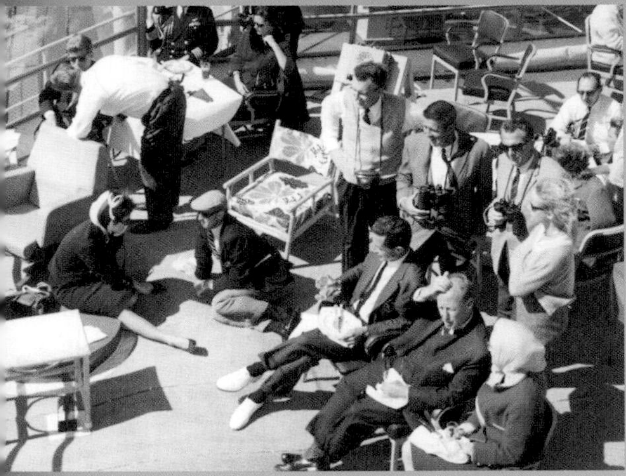

Jackie converses with an unidentified man while sitting on the deck of the *Kennedy*. A little over a month later, the USS *Kennedy* would be in the Caribbean participating in the blockade of Cuba during the Cuban Missile Crisis.

Jack and Jackie share a private moment in the midst of the crowd on the deck. When they came aboard, they were welcomed in a ceremony in which the crew presented them a model of the ship.

The highlight came when Jack, Jackie, and a plethora of guests and dignitaries watched the America's Cup races from the deck of the USS *Joseph P. Kennedy Jr.* History was made as the deck of the *Kennedy* was smattered with tables covered with white tablecloths and accompanied by a full bar—a first for the U.S. Navy. It was "absolutely divine...And Jack was in absolute heaven...he really did love the Navy and love the sea." [180] Jackie also enjoyed her time aboard the *Kennedy*, especially the wide range of guests from across the American landscape of art, culture, and power.

The Newport vacation came to an end with the welcoming of an old friend. Ayub Khan returned and was received for a luncheon at Hammersmith Farm, just as his Indian counterpart Nehru had been a summer before. Jackie's March trip to India and Pakistan was a smashing success in both countries. Well received by both Nehru and his people, Jackie developed a deep interest in Indian art and architecture. Nehru appreciated Jackie's company, as she was "an American not obliged to talk about politics" [181] and one with an interest in Indian art, its culture, and its people.

However, Jackie had developed a special connection with Khan. Initially born of a shared love of equestrian pursuits, she came to find him "like Jack...magnificent in his uniform...tough and brave and wants things done in a hurry." [182] Over 400,000 Pakistanis lined the streets of the capital city of Rawalpindi waving paper flags and signs reading, "Long live Mrs. Kennedy." Virtually everyone who lived in the city was present for what was "the biggest welcome ever given a foreign visitor." [183] Khan presented her with a ten-year-old bay gelding named Sadar, which was flown home in a military plane to be ridden by Jackie at Middleburg.

Jackie and Jack flew to Washington that evening, and the following day Jackie and Khan rode across the Virginia countryside together, her upon Sadar while Khan rode Jackie's horse Minbreno.

It was Saturday morning June 22, 1963, three days following Medgar Evers's burial in Arlington National Cemetery. President Kennedy held separate meetings with NAACP director Roy Wilkins and then with thirty-four-year-old Martin Luther King Jr. In just two months King would forge his place in history, professing his dream on the steps of the Lincoln Memorial. Another meeting followed as James Farmer, Whitney Young, A. Philip Randolph and John Lewis joined Wilkins, King, and twenty-five others discussing the fight for integration.

The president spent the afternoon at Camp David with Jackie and the kids before boarding Air Force I at 9:35 p.m. for a flight to Germany. He would visit Germany, Ireland, England, and Italy before returning home for the Fourth of July in Hyannis Port. What awaited him was the most electrifying moment of the entire Kennedy administration and a visit to his ancestral homeland, which Jack would refer to as "the three happiest days...in my life."[184]

Jackie, nearing thirty weeks pregnant, dined in Georgetown with Secretary of Defense Robert McNamara before returning to the White House, where they watched replays of Jack's speech at the Berlin Wall. Virtually every one of the 2.5 million citizens of West Berlin came out to see the president, either cheering on the motorcade route waving and chanting, "Ken a dee, Ken a dee, Ken a dee," or as part of the 1.5 million who gathered in the square to hear him speak from in front of the wall. Standing with West Berlin mayor Willy Brandt, Jack's speech culminated in one of his most famous lines when he closed with: "All free men, wherever they may live, are citizens of Berlin. Therefore as a free man I take pride in the words, *Ich bin ein Berliner* [I am a Berliner]."

As Jack was being welcomed in his ancestral home, Jackie was flying from Washington, D.C., to Newport and Hammersmith. A photo of a smiling Jack, standing in a car as it motorcaded through the streets of Cork, occupied the front page of the *Newport Daily News.* Just below, a short story declared, "Mrs. Kennedy Here for a Visit." While the eyes and ears of the world were on President Kennedy and his rousing speech at the Berlin Wall, Jackie was in "her favorite place...the deck room," where ceiling-to-floor glass windows afforded a spectacular view of Hammersmith' s emerald green lawn running to the shores of Narragansett Bay. It was in this room that she sat painting and listening while members of the Auchincloss crew watched news footage of Jack, espousing the virtues of freedom.[185] Following a few quiet days and a couple of trips to Pitcher's Drug Store for ice cream cones, Jackie and the kids headed for Hyannis to await both Jack and the Fourth of July.

Expecting her baby at the end of August, Jackie settled in at Brambletyde, their Squaw Island home. It was the third Cape Cod summer home for the first family, with each one affording them more privacy. The plan was to remain there throughout the summer, returning to Washington for a C-section delivery at Walter Reed Hospital. Gifts and letters to Jackie were being received at the White House—about three hundred per day. Arriving from all over the world, they included bibs, bonnets, sweaters, and homemade quilts. Some were suggestions for names, others offers to be godparents, and some even suggested that she have the baby at the White House. With still eight weeks until her due date, more than one hundred gifts had been received. Jackie released a statement informing all that the gifts would be donated to charitable organizations and also declared that only gifts under fifteen dollars would be accepted. With Jackie's history of premature births, the hospital at nearby Otis Air Force Base was being prepared for that possibility.

Jackie also announced that she was breaking with her policy of not endorsing any programs outside Washington, D.C., and Newport became the benefactor. She lent her name as an honorary patron of "Newport Weekends," a newly formed group dedicated to bring top musical programs to Newport's Van Alen Casino Theater through Labor Day. This was not a random choice, for Jackie's patronage of "Newport Weekends" combined her passion for music, the arts, historical restoration, and preservation. After being closed for several years, the Newport Casino reopened on July 11, 1963, with Mrs. Kennedy listed as its "honorary patron."

The joyful anticipation of the baby's birth turned to unspeakable heartache when Patrick Bouvier Kennedy was born on August 7 and died just two days later. In the aftermath of Patrick's death and through the profound sadness and depression that followed, two significant family events took place. The first was the revelry of the Kennedy patriarch's seventy-fifth birthday. Grampy Joe was surrounded by his offspring and twenty-one grandchildren. There was gaiety and laughter as the kids gave Grampy gag gifts and sang to him. As the day turned to evening, Jack sang to his father "September Song," a Kennedy favorite and a staple at family gatherings: "Oh the days dwindle down, to a precious few, September, November. And these few precious days I'll spend with you." [186] It was a poignant juxtaposition—Grampy Joe

Jackie arrives at the entrance to the Elms in September 1962. Completed in 1901 for coal baron Edward Berwind, it was nearly destroyed after his niece Julia died in 1961. The Newport Preservation Society purchased it in the nick of time in July 1962, saving it from the wrecking ball.

celebrating his seventy-fifth year one month removed from the birth and death of his grandson, who lived but thirty-nine hours. "That was a killer," Martha Bartlett recalled. "The old man in a wheelchair, the son singing." And, Bartlett added, "you almost felt, Jack knew he wasn't going to see old age."[187]

The gray skies and chilly breeze of this precious September weekend did not prevent Jack and Jackie from cruising Lewis Bay aboard the *Honey Fitz*. It is serendipitous that on the last weekend of Jack and Jackie's last summer together, Charlie and Martha Bartlett, the two who brought them together, would be their guests. They talked of the possibility of Bobby running for president in 1968 and thought he would have to fight Lyndon Johnson for the nomination. They also mused at what they might do upon leaving the

Jackie unveils the model for the National Center for the Arts. Present were: Geraldine Page (blue dress, brown cover) and Danny Kaye (right). Partially obscured by flash on the right are Paul Newman and his wife Joanne Woodward. Janet Auchincloss is behind Jackie. The center would become the John F. Kennedy Center for the Performing Arts.

White House. Jackie joked that she had no interest in being "the wife of a headmaster of a girl's school." Although not happy with the barb, Jack told Charlie that he was thinking about being the ambassador to Italy because "Jackie would like it."[188]

On September 12, Jack and Jackie's tenth anniversary, Jackie, Caroline, and John Jr. boarded a helicopter on Grampy Joe's Hyannis Port front lawn for the forty-minute ride to Hammersmith's back lawn. Jack was scheduled to arrive from Washington at 6:30 p.m., and then they would celebrate an intimate dinner at Hammersmith Farm commemorating their first decade of marriage. Jackie was feeling better physically, but the loss of Patrick weighed heavily on her. She had experienced post-partum depression before, and this time it was heightened exponentially by Patrick's death. With Janet's encouragement, Jackie was poised to do her best to make the weekend a happy one.

Flying with Jack on Air Force I were old Georgetown friends Ben and Toni Bradlee and two of the Kennedy family dogs, a cocker spaniel named Shannon and a wolf hound named Wolf, both given to the president by the people of Ireland. The Bradlees were joining Jack and Jackie for their anniversary celebration. It was 6:37 p.m. when Air Force I touched down at Quonset. The Marine I helicopter was waiting, and Jack told Ben and Toni to wait in the helicopter, as he had to do a "little toe dance" with Rhode Island's Republican governor John Chafee. About five hundred people were gathered for the president's "toe dance,"[189] which consisted of a ten-minute ceremony.

The setting New England sun cast a yellow glow across the emerald lawn and upon Hammersmith's shingled mansion. In a scene Bradlee described as "half space age pomp and half *Wuthering Heights*," the chopper landed on the lawn. It was the first time the Bradlees had seen Jackie since Patrick's death, and Bradlee noted that Jack and Jackie greeted each other with "by far the most affectionate embrace we had ever seen them give each other."[190] "When he arrived at Hammersmith Farm," Janet remembered, "he landed in the helicopter in the field...we all walked out to meet him."[191] The "we" included "Uncle Hugh," Jackie's step-brother Yusha, and Sylvia (Whitehouse) Blake, who had been one of Jackie's bridesmaids, as well as Jackie's Auchincloss sister Janet and brother Jamie, also members of the wedding party. "Then we walked back together."[192]

Cocktails were served in the deck room just as they had been ten years earlier. Jack loved daiquiris, and so did his father-in-law, Hugh. Yusha took charge of the bar, informing Jack that "instead of two different kinds of rum, why don't we have a light rum, a medium rum and a dark rum." Jack concurred and dubbed the drink the "New Frontier."[193]

During cocktails the couple opened their gifts, with the highlight coming when they gifted each other. Jack read a letter from New York antique dealer J.J. Klejman, which included a list of in-stock items available for purchase. Jackie could choose whichever item she wanted. Each came with a description and a price. Jack read the descriptions, and although he did not read the prices aloud, he would whisper to the Bradlees, "We'll have to steer her away from that one," when he came upon a particularly expensive item.[194] Among the items were statues and Etruscan art objects from the second century BCE, Egyptian necklaces, and a Thai bracelet.

Jackie, in her spirit of true historian and historical restorer, gave to Jack a scrapbook of the White House Rose Garden. It contained before and after photos of the garden, which their mutual friend Bunny Mellon had created for him. On each photo page Jackie placed a copy of Jack's schedule for that particular day. Jackie then added a quotation in her own hand, many of them from columnist Joseph Alsop's gardening column. Jack read all the quotes, "pausing to admire Joe's ornate prose."[195]

Janet recalled it was "a happy sort of evening. I felt that they were closer. They'd certainly been through as much as people can go through together in ten years: tragedy and joy...Their children's births and deaths... I can't think of two people who had packed more into ten years of marriage than they had. And I felt that all their strains and stresses, which any sensitive people have in a marriage, had eased to a point where they were terribly close to each other…I think one felt in those rare moments when one could be alone with them on a quiet evening when there weren't a million pressures pending—that they were very, very, very close to each other and understood each other wonderfully. He appreciated her gifts and she worshiped him and appreciated his humor and his kindness, and they really had fun together." [196]

The following morning the Bradlees joined Jack for the ride over to Quonset, where he was filming a message. Jackie would meet them at Fort Adams for a *Honey Fitz* luncheon cruise. On the road to Fort Adams, the president's car was stopped behind a school bus. Jack watched as a young girl wearing braces on her legs got off. Jack got out of the car, bounded to the bus, and hopped aboard. "Hello children, how are you?" he said, walking down the aisle and greeting each one of them. "One girl named Martha was so excited, she almost jumped from her braces." It turned out that he had come upon fourteen kids, aged five through twelve, who were handicapped and or mentally challenged. After greeting them all, he bade them adieu and continued on his trip, leaving "the happiest children in all Newport."[197]

It was on to Fort Adams, where Jackie, Yusha, Senator Claiborne Pell, his wife Nuala, and even the cocker spaniel Shannon joined them for lunch. Shannon spent her time curled up quietly on a seat at the stern. Following a lunch of chowder, fettuccini Alfredo, burgers, and, of course, ice cream, they returned to the house for a quick refresh, and then it was over to the Newport Country Club for ninety minutes of golf. Saturday was more of the same, with a stop added for a dip in the pool at Bailey's Beach. It was a chilly weekend, but Jack and John Jr. were undaunted as both went in for a swim. Jack placed John Jr. in a life preserver and pulled him through the water as Jackie sat poolside thumbing through a magazine.

Following the 10:00 a.m. mass at St. Mary's, Jackie, Caroline, and John Jr. went to Bailey's Beach with Ben and Toni Bradlee. Jackie sat on the seawall while the kids dug in the sand. Toni and Ben walked the beach while Jack and John strolled towards the shore. An empty rowboat sat in the sand, and they climbed in. Sitting side by side Jack showed his smiling little boy how to maneuver the oars. John found the line more interesting, and playing with it, he slid in front of his daddy, leaning into him. Jack wrapped his arms around him, embracing both his love of his little boy and his love of the sea.

The weekend boosted Jackie's spirits, and she was feeling strong enough to accept Lee's invitation to sail with her in Greece aboard Aristotle Onassis' yacht, *Christina*. The two-week trip was slated for the first of October. Although not enamored with the idea, Jack thought it would be good for her. When the trip came to an end, Jackie told Clint Hill, "You know Mr.

On Sunday, September 15, 1963, Jack and John walked on Bailey's Beach and climbed into this rowboat. Dad was showing John how to hold the oars, and he became more interested in the line. Gathering it up, he leaned into his father prompting a hug. Toni and Ben Bradlee walk in the background.

Jackie and Jack head up an unspecified fairway towards a gray sky as their anniversary weekend draws to a close, two months prior to their trip to Texas.

Hill, the president is going on a trip to Texas next month and he wants me to join him. I didn't think I was ready. But now I'm feeling so much better and I really want to help him as much as I can. Maybe I will go after all." [198]

In what would turn out to be the last weekend that Hammersmith Farm served as the summer White House, Jack and Jackie orchestrated a playful, prophetic prank. Directing a Laurel and Hardyish dark comedy with White House photographer Robert Knudsen behind the camera, the production became ironically chilling and sadly a tragic foreshadowing of the immediate future.

Friday, September 20, 1963, began for the president at the United Nations, where he called for nuclear disarmament talks and the possibility of a joint Soviet/U.S. expedition to the moon. It ended when Marine I touched down on the Hammersmith lawn at 6:20 p.m. Paul "Red" Fay and his family, as well as Countess Crespi and her son, were joining the first family.

The weekend was sporadically overcast and cool, but it did not dissuade the clan from the beach or the water. Both days included trips to Bailey's Beach, the sand, the pool, and the boat. Jackie sat on the seawall while Caroline, John, and their pals dug, shoveled, and played with trucks in the sand. "Red" Fay and John John splashed heartily in the pool as Fay threw him repeatedly into the air from the water, eliciting giggles each time. The afternoons brought the treasured cruises aboard the *Honey Fitz*.

Sunday afternoon's cruise found Jackie's spirits high for the first time since Patrick's death six weeks earlier. "Red" and Jack reminisced, Jack read palms, the cocktails flowed, and the kids played along the deck as Knudsen filmed and photoed. While out on the bay, Jackie and Jack concocted a sequence for a film, the script of which Jack had actually "written," inspired by his love and fascination with and for James Bond novels. [199] Jack assigned everybody a role, and upon their return to the dock, the action began. The president was walking down the long pier toward Hammersmith Farm when he suddenly clutched his chest and fell. Unaffected, Countess Crespi and her son simply stepped over him. Jackie followed, equally unmoved, and daintily stepped around him. Behind her was "Red" Fay, who tripped and fell on top of the president, and as he did, "a gush of red surged from the president's mouth,"[200] spilling down the front of his shirt.

The Secret Service contingent was waiting at the dock. Jackie, windblown and with the color of the sun in her cheeks, approached agent Roy Kellerman. "Mr. Kellerman," she asked, "would you please do us a favor?" "What do you need Mrs. Kennedy," said the accommodating agent. "We're making a film about the president's murder, and we'd like you and the other agents to drive up to the front of the house, then jump out and run toward the door."

The agents were a bit taken aback, yet despite the outlandish request, to a man, they were happy to see her so relaxed and enjoying herself. "You want us to drive up now?" asked Kellerman. "No, just as soon as Mr. Knudsen is ready," came her excited answer, and she bounded back to the group.[201] With the president at the wheel of the Lincoln convertible, Jackie slid in next to him. Caroline, Sally Fay, and Brando Crespi climbed up the trunk of the car and perched themselves on the top of the backseat. "Red" and Anita slipped into the backseat, the countess got in next to Jackie. Then they were off, with the Secret Service car in tow. All the agents donned their shades, ready to play their role under Jackie's direction.

To the delight of the kids, it was a short, bumpy ride up the dirt road to the house, and when the car came to a stop at the front door, they slid off the trunk and ran, yelling and laughing, into the house. Everybody grabbed something from the car to bring inside. Jackie remained with Knudsen, and with the kids safely inside, the filming commenced.

Knudsen directed the agents to "drive the car up from the command post and pull up to the front of the house and make a mad dash for the door." "Look desperate, like you heard shots," Jackie added, "and are concerned that the president might be hurt and you need to respond fast." Gerald Blaine drove back down the dirt road, turned, and headed back up. Approaching, he floored the gas pedal, spinning tires and kicking up dust, before slamming on the brakes and bringing the car to a screeching halt right at the front door. They jumped out of the car and ran to the front door. Clapping her hands, Jackie said to Knudsen, "That was great, did you get it?"

"Got it," he said. "Great action sequence." Jackie thanked the agents for their efforts before the two of them went inside.[202]

Four times, Knudsen filmed the sequence, with Fay twice playing the victim. White House reporters Merriman Smith and Frank Cormier were following the *Honey Fitz* in a speedboat, watching through binoculars. They witnessed the sequence in which Fay fell upon the deck and reported that Fay had "stretched prone on the long pier…clowning with Mr. Kennedy for the benefit of a government photographer." The sequence ended with Jack walking down the pier as he "laughingly put his foot on Mr. Fay's stomach."[203] In another sequence Fay played the role of Crespi's "ardent suitor." Wearing "the least conservative and most colorful" bikini, chosen by Jack, Crespi sprinted across the Hammersmith lawn. Fay, wearing long boxer shorts and garters, was in hot pursuit. "Crespi give him a chance!" yelled Jack across the lawn as the couple ended up "horizontal in the bushes…with a close up of Fay's feet sticking out of Mrs. Auchincloss' Queen Elizabeth rose bushes."[204]

Robert Knudsen confirmed the story and said the sequence had been shot several times. "There were about four other couples there," Knudsen said. "They thought it would be kind of fun to do it. There was a little dialogue, but I'm not about to repeat it. It was done in confidence, and even though he's dead, it's still in confidence."[205] The film is at the JFK Library but remains closed for viewing.

On November 1, the White House confirmed that "President and Mrs. Kennedy have leased Annandale Farm on Ridge Road for next August and September."[206] However, Jack and Jackie would never return to Hammersmith Farm or Newport. Jack's weekends found him in California, Camp David, and in Massachusetts while Jackie journeyed to Greece. They spent the first two November weekends at their new home in Middleton, Virginia, which Jackie called Atoka. Jack then traveled to Cape Canaveral, and the next week Jackie joined him for a campaign swing scheduled through five Texas cities in two days before spending the night at LBJ's Ranch.

Then it would be home for John's birthday, then Caroline's, before heading on to the Cape and the Kennedy traditional Thanksgiving gathering in Hyannis Port.

# PART III

# *Mr. and Mrs. America*

"Ebullient joy...unutterable pathos...unspeakable sadness."

*Texas Congressman James Wright*

Jack Kennedy dressed and went downstairs to the Oval Office. He had one order of business before leaving for Texas: a five-minute meeting with two ambassadors. The meeting ended, and he returned upstairs where Kenneth, Jackie's hairdresser, was putting the finishing touches on her hair. "Are you ready?" the president asked. "The helicopter is waiting." [207] With John in tow, they made their way downstairs to the South Lawn and Marine I. Watching them, Kenneth thought "there was none of the strain that I sometimes had seen...before important state dinners and things like that. They look marvelously happy together, as happy and close as I've ever seen them." [208]

Making her way up the steps to the aircraft, Jackie glanced toward John, who was crying when they left him, hoping he'd settled down. He loved riding in the helicopter, which was always enough to overcome his sadness at saying goodbyes. Today his tears were unabated and his sadness not assuaged. In four days he would be three years old.

The historic Texas trip was underway. It marked the first time in the history of the Lone Star State that a president appeared for a fundraising event. It was also the first time that a president, vice-president, and governor of Texas would appear on the same program. For Jackie, it marked her first visit to Texas and the first time she had ever accompanied her husband on a presidential political tour.

She sat with her secretary working on a speech as Air Force I approached its final descent to Brooks Air Force Base in San Antonio, Texas. Across the table her husband, glasses perched on his nose, read from the folder marked "EYES ONLY PRESIDENT."[209]

Jackie chats with Caroline who's just returned from a swim in the ocean off the side of the *Honey Fitz* in August 1963. Jackie is 35 weeks pregnant with Patrick and three days away from an emergency C-section.

It was November 21, 1963, and it had been 105 days since the emergency C-section birth of Patrick Bouvier Kennedy. On that day, August 7, Jackie and Caroline had just arrived at Allen Farm for Caroline's riding lesson. They had barely arrived when Jackie turned to Landis and said, "Mr. Landis, I think we should get back to the compound right now...we better hurry." With the first lady imploring him to "please go a little faster," [210] Landis traversed the winding roads of Cape Cod at eighty miles per hour. Reaching the compound, they immediately boarded a helicopter bound for the hospital at Otis Air Force Base. Nearly six weeks from her due date, the level of anxiety was high, for this was her fifth pregnancy. The births of Caroline and John had been preceded by a miscarriage and a stillborn birth.

In Washington, President Kennedy walked into the office of his secretary, Evelyn Lincoln. She was on the phone with the Kennedy home on the Cape. "Mrs. Kennedy is on her way to Otis," she informed the president. Kennedy placed two quick calls to Hyannis Port before calling Air Force aide General McHugh with instructions to prepare a flight north. He scribbled a couple of notes, folded the papers, and put them in his pocket as he made his way to the helicopter on the South Lawn. With neither presidential plane available, the presidential party boarded a small charter plane, and as this crowded, diminutive version of Air Force I winged its way north, an uncharacteristic silence permeated the air. President Kennedy took a seat, and "he just kept staring out the window," remembered Jackie's press secretary Pam Turnure, "and obviously his thoughts were completely with her...it was a very quiet trip." [211] Twenty-two minutes into the flight, Jackie gave birth to a four-pound, ten-ounce baby boy.

Dr. John Walsh emerged from surgery and informed Jackie's Secret Service agent, Clint Hill, "You can breathe easy. Mrs. Kennedy has delivered a baby boy and she is doing fine."

"How's the baby," Hill responded, noting a disquieted look in the doctor's eyes.

"He's small. We have some concern about his breathing. We've put him in an incubator, and we'll know more in a while."

"I'll make sure the president gets the news immediately," Hill told the doctor. "He's on his way and he should be here soon." [212]

It was 1:40 p.m. when the president arrived. "Congratulations, Mr. President," said Clint Hill.

"Thank you. How's Mrs. Kennedy?" came his quick reply.

"I believe she's still under sedation, but you should talk to Dr. Walsh."

Jack went to see his wife, and after a short conference with Walsh, he instructed Clint Hill to "find the base chaplain. We need to baptize the baby right away." [213]

The president then placed a call to Kennedy family obstetrician Dr. Roy Heffernan. "Doctor," the president went right to the point, "Jackie has just had a little boy, and he isn't doing well. He has some respiratory difficulty. Would you kindly find the best man…to deal with this sort of situation, and I'll have a plane at Logan Airport waiting for him, and he can come right down here. I would be grateful if you would do this." [214]

In a matter of minutes Dr. James E. Drorbaugh was in a chopper bound for Otis Air Force Base. The president was waiting for Drorbaugh and immediately took him to examine Patrick. Finding him in moderate distress, "with a rapid respiratory rate, with grunting and lots of effort going into each breath," he recommended Patrick be transferred to Boston Children's Hospital. [215]

Jackie spent most of her afternoon in recovery, drifting in and out of sleep, catching but "brief glimpses of her new son." The last one came when her husband "wheeled him into her room in a special incubator." [216] She reached into the incubator and for ten minutes stroked his hair and held his tiny little hand, never knowing that this would be the measure of their lives together. Patrick was then placed in an ambulance bound for Boston.

Just before 6:00 p.m., Jack and his sister Jean boarded Marine I for the short flight to the first family's summer home on Squaw Island and a visit with Caroline and John. Jack then returned to Jackie before he was back in the chopper on his way to Otis and an awaiting plane to Boston. He arrived at the Boston Children's Hospital just after 9:00 p.m., conferred with the doctors, and visited little Patrick before retiring to the Kennedy apartment at the Ritz Carlton, ten minutes away.

The baby was suffering from hyaline membrane disease. Now called Infant Respiratory Distress Syndrome (IRDS), it is a structural immaturity of the lungs in premature births. John Jr. suffered the same affliction, and the first forty-eight hours were critical. The country, and indeed the world, now shared the vigil of President and Mrs. Kennedy.

After breakfast with appointment secretary and longtime friend Kenny O'Donnell, the president went back to the hospital. Receiving encouraging news, he returned to Otis for an hour-long visit with Jackie. Patrick showed some improvement, fueling the hope that he could endure the respiratory malady as John had three years earlier. Although she would spend most of the day sleeping, Jackie did open congratulatory offerings and perused some newspaper articles regarding the arrival of her second son. Carrying the burden of his harbored concern, Jack protected Jackie from the severity of Patrick's condition, preferring to provide hope fostered by the morning's encouraging signs. At noon it was back to the kids on Squaw Island.

A call soon came from Boston. The encouraging signs of the morning had dissipated, and Patrick was being placed in a hyperbaric chamber to force oxygen into his tiny little lungs. Jack called Jackie's mom in Newport and then was back on Marine I bound for Logan Airport, where he met Janet Auchincloss and headed for the hospital.

Twice he donned surgical gown and mask to visit with Patrick. He would slide his hand inside to simply hold his son's tiny little fingers. At one point he turned to Janet and said, "Nothing must happen to Patrick, because I just can't bear to think of the effect it might have on Jackie." It was unmistakably clear to Janet "the effect it might have on him too."[217]

Following an 8:25 p.m. doctor's conference, Jack decided to spend the night at the hospital. A fourth-floor room was procured, adding a cot for Special Assistant Dave Powers. Powers, a member of the Irish mafia, had been with Jack from the start. It was just after 2:00 a.m. when Secret Service agent Gerry Behn woke Powers, informing him Patrick had taken a turn for the worse.

Dave awakened the president, conveying the sad news, and as the pair paced awaiting the elevator, Jack walked by a room in the intensive care unit. Inside lay a small child who had been severely burned. He called the nurse, asking the details of the incident. He then inquired about the mother. "How often does she visit?" he asked.

Patrick lived only 39 hours, of which Jackie spent only minutes with him. She remained hospitalized following surgery and was unable to attend his funeral. Here press secretary Pierre Salinger announces Patrick's death to the press, outside the hospital at Otis Air Force Base.

"Every day," said the nurse.

"Can you tell me her name?"[218] Jack then turned to Powers, who handed him paper and pen. Completing a short note of sympathy and encouragement for an anguished parent, he handed it to the nurse.

Donning the surgical cap and gown, Jack reached into the hyperbaric chamber and grasped the tiny fingers of his dying son. There he remained, watching and hoping against hope, as Patrick battled for each breath. At 4:04 a.m. on August 9, 1963, in the thirty-ninth hour of his life, Patrick Bouvier Kennedy's battle ended. He drew his last breath while his daddy held his hand. "He put up quite a fight," Jack said. "He was a beautiful baby."[219]

The president and Powers returned to their room, and Jack turned to his old friend. "Would you go outside and call Teddy," he asked, and as Powers left the room, the president sat on his bed and wept. "He didn't want anybody to see him cry," recalled Powers.[220]

Gerry Behn called Otis informing Clint Hill and Tom Wells that Patrick had passed away. Wells then called Dr. Walsh, notifying him of Patrick's passing and the president's request that he tell Jackie. The Kennedys joined the John Adamses, the Jeffersons, the Lincolns, and the Coolidges on the unenviable list of families who lost children while occupying the White House.

The day at Otis had been a beehive of activity, with phone calls and messages pouring in from all over the world, expressing concerns about the plight of baby Patrick. Jackie, still recuperating, slept on and off throughout most of it, still not totally aware of the gravity of her baby's condition.

The night proved to be a fitful one for Jackie, with Nurse Lumsden coming in and out of her room throughout. "Mrs. Kennedy is really having a tough time tonight," Lumsden said to Agent Wells. "She's been so restless all night, tossing and turning. She just can't seem to get to sleep." At just after 4:00 a.m. Nurse Lumsden emerged from Jackie Kennedy's room. "She's finally gone to sleep," she told Tom Wells. "She just fell asleep." [221] It was within minutes of Patrick's passing.

In the predawn hours Jack placed a call to Cardinal Cushing, and the two old friends planned a mass of the angels to be said the following day at the cardinal's residence in Brighton, Massachusetts. The task of executing the plans went to longtime aide Frank Morrissey. "I remember Bobby calling, with the arrangements to be made." Morrissey made his way over to Cushing's residence, where the cardinal had decorated the altar himself. "We had to go with the undertaker, George Lacy, we got a beautiful little gown... all in white." A vault was flown in from Cleveland, and baby Patrick was now ready to be laid to rest. [222]

Dr. Walsh arrived at 6:30 p.m. to deliver the crushing news to Jackie, and it devastated her. Mary Gallagher, Nancy Tuckerman, Pam Turnure, and Nurse Luella Hennessey provided as much comfort and support as possible, but it was impossible to know the palpable anguish that saturated her soul. It was her fifth pregnancy in eight years and her third lost child.

Being thoroughly protected by the president left Jackie unprepared for the news of Patrick's death. She did not know that he only had a fifty-fifty chance from the moment he arrived. She did not know that the first forty-eight hours would be critical. She did not know of, nor see, her husband's utter torment as he powerlessly watched his tiny little boy battle for breath. She did not see the gentle tenderness that emerged from Jack as friends and staff alike witnessed a side of him they had not seen before. His emotions were raw and exposed, heard in his voice, seen on his face, and visible in his eyes. His stoic, protective demeanor, shown to Jackie throughout, left her to wonder if it marked the same indifference with which he had greeted the stillborn birth of Arabella seven years earlier.

One can only wonder if her mind wandered back to the summer of 1956. It was but days after the Democratic Convention in which her husband had lost his bid to land the second spot on the ticket with Adlai Stevenson. Jack was off on a pleasure trip to sail the European coast, accompanied by Senator George Smathers, Congressman and former Harvard classmate Torbet MacDonald, and younger brother Teddy.

Jackie had returned home to Newport and Hammersmith Farm. A little over seven months pregnant, she was left behind while Jack cavorted, gallivanting about the Mediterranean, enjoying wine, women, and more women.

Did she recall her first engagement to John Husted and ponder how things might have been had she chosen him instead of Jack? Or perhaps she remembered a conversation with Lemoyne Billings, her husband's friend since their junior high school days at the Choate School in Connecticut?

It was the night of the first Inaugural Ball of Dwight Eisenhower. Before the ball, Jack and his sister Pat hosted a cocktail party at their home in Georgetown. Billings took this opportunity to talk with Jackie about her pending nuptials to the country's most eligible bachelor.

The thirty-five-year-old senator was "crazy about girls, but he never really settled down with one girl...He was terribly interested in going out and having fun with them at night." He was never really "terribly excited about having girls as friends." As his wedding approached he was "worried about the responsibilities he was taking on as a husband...he was scared." Billings sought out twenty-three-year-old Jacqueline Bouvier, for he "had known Jack a long time...and I felt as if I should prepare her a little bit for what I felt were some of the problems that Jack might have in marrying at thirty-five. She was terribly young and it might be best if she were prepared for it."[223]

Billings minced few words in relating his friend's predilection and penchant for women. And in this prenuptial conversation with this "awfully pretty girl, younger and prettier girl than most he dated," he delicately informed her that she should not expect it to stop after they were married. "Jack...has been around an awful lot in his life...known many, many girls...

You're going to have to be very understanding at the beginning...he never really settled down with one girl before...A man of thirty-five is very hard to live with."[224]

Twenty-three-year-old Miss Bouvier soaked in the words of Jack's longest and most loyal friend. "She was very understanding" and "accepted everything I said," recalled Billings. Jackie would re-visit this conversation with Billings after their marriage, telling him, "I realized all that and I thought it was a challenge."[225]

On August 24, 1956, the front page of the *Newport Daily News* reported, "Senator Kennedy's Wife Under Knife, Loses Her Baby." Mrs. Kennedy was rushed to Newport Hospital after "she suffered an internal hemorrhage... the former Miss Jacqueline Lee Bouvier was visiting her step-father and mother Mr. and Mrs. Hugh D Auchincloss at Hammersmith Farm" when the incident took place, and "the emergency operation was performed at 7 p.m....Family members today were seeking to reach Senator Kennedy, who is sailing with his brother Edward Kennedy off France...and is due in port sometime today."

Four days later, the *Newport Daily News* reported that Jack "arrived at 1:15 p.m. today after an air trip from Italy...He took a transatlantic plane to Boston today and immediately went aboard a chartered plane for Newport." He was unreachable as "he was cruising off the coast of Italy and had not been aware of his wife's illness." Fortunately, he sent a "routine cable from Portofino, Italy," which allowed his "exact location" to be learned. The cold, harsh reality was quite different.

On the afternoon of August 23, 1956, Jackie was awakened from an afternoon nap bleeding and in excruciating pain. Her placenta had separated prematurely, causing the early onset of the birth process and taking the life of the baby girl she held within. Within a half hour she was in an ambulance speeding through the streets of Newport, bound for Newport Hospital. With Jackie's life now endangered, an emergency Caesarean section was performed. Janet placed a call to Hyannis Port to learn that Jack was inaccessible. When Jackie awoke at 2:00 a.m., it was Bobby she found at her bedside. It was Bobby who told her that she had given birth to a beautiful baby girl, and it was Bobby who told her that the girl they would have called Arabella had been born dead.

Where was Jack? He was off sailing on a yacht with three buddies and enough women to go around. When word reached Jack's secretary, Evelyn Lincoln, of Jackie's plight and their stillborn baby, she placed a call to Jack, who said he'd "be right home." However, in a moment of incalculable poor judgment, he reached the conclusion that "if I go back there what the hell am I going to do, I'm just going to sit there and ring my hands." His callous disregard of Jackie's grief and desolation caused one *Washington Post* reporter to write of "his terrible obtuseness, his willful insensitivity." This prompted friend and fellow traveler George Smathers to offer, "If you want to run for president, you'd better get your ass back to your wife's bedside, or else every wife in the country will be against you."[226]

Before Jack returned, Bobby, along with Kenny O'Donnell, stood graveside while the tiny coffin marked "Baby Girl Kennedy" was lowered into the earth in St. Columba's Cemetery, overlooking Narragansett Bay.

When Jack arrived, Jackie was awash in a cauldron of emotions: heartache, anger, self-recrimination, despair, and all stops in between. For all of the warnings she had received from Lem Billings on that January night four years earlier, nothing had prepared her for the depth of the indignity which Jack's cruel insensitivity placed on her through this crushing ordeal. All the fears she'd expressed to Father Leonard—he's "like my father," "loves the chase," "bored with the conquest," "flirts," "resents you," "it nearly killed mummy"—were now her reality.

Patrick's death devastated Jackie, leaving her inconsolable and unable to stop the tears. Just before 9:00 p.m., Mary Gallagher informed her that the president was on his way. Not sure what to expect, Jackie wanted to put on her best face. Physically weak and emotionally drained, Mary and Luella assisted her, helping wash her face, comb her hair, and propping her up on the bed. There was nothing they could do to touch the sorrowful ache of her soul.

Thirty minutes later, "looking like he had been to hell and back," President Kennedy approached his wife's room. "My condolences Mr. President," said Clint Hill as he turned the door knob, allowing him to enter.

"Thanks, Clint," said the exhausted, heart-broken chief executive as he passed through the door.[227] "He walked… in my room and just sobbed and put his arms around me." In all the time she'd known him, she had seen tears fall from his eyes only twice before. The first time was when he underwent back surgery in their first year of marriage; "he wouldn't weep but some tears would fill his eyes and roll down his cheek." The second time occurred with the realization that the Bay of Pigs invasion had turned to an ultimate disaster, and "he came over…to his bedroom…just put his head in his hands and sort of wept."[228]

Today it was far beyond simply tears. It was the gut-wrenching sobs that emanate from the soul when sadness reaches to the core of one's being. Jack and Jackie spent two hours in that room. Emotionally guarded through ten years of marriage, they melted together in a sadness only they could know.

Jack then hopped aboard Marine I, bound for Squaw Island, where his children awaited him. Throughout the summer, they had been anticipating the arrival of a new baby, and it now fell upon their dad to tell them that Patrick would not be coming home. "John was not old enough to take in too much," recalled nanny Maud Shaw, but Caroline completely understood what her dad meant when he told her that Patrick "had been sick and he had gone to heaven." He spent the afternoon with his children, consoling Caroline and reveling in his little boy. Twice he returned to visit with Jackie, and he squeezed in a twenty-minute visit with his dad before returning home at just before 11:00 p.m.

The day, which had begun twenty-one hours earlier when Dave Powers awakened him with the words, "Patrick's taken a turn for the worse," was finally over.

The following morning three helicopters left Hyannis Port filled with Kennedys, Auchinclosses, and a few close intimates to lay little Patrick to rest. Too weak and still sedated, Jackie did not attend. The thirty-minute mass was said in "the little chapel in the Archbishop's residence." The chapel emptied, and only the cardinal and the president remained. "I saw tears in the eyes of Jack Kennedy and they were copious tears," Cardinal Cushing remembered. "I was right behind him...The casket was there...in a white marble case. The president was overwhelmed with grief. He literally put his arm around the casket as though he was carrying it out."

"Come on Jack," said the priest to his friend. "Let's go. God is good."[229]

At Holyhood Cemetery another lamentable scene unfolded. Secret Service agent Gerald Blaine recalled, "The agents, who prided themselves on hiding their emotions, wept openly as they watched President Kennedy's shoulders heave up and down with deep heavy sobs as the tiny white coffin was placed in the ground."[230] For Jackie it was a day of isolated heartache. Still recuperating and under sedation, she struggled to simply keep her composure.

Longtime friend David Ormsby Gore characterized Jack as one with "deep emotions" who "very much disliked the display of them" and for whom "public displays was anathema."[231] Janet observed of Jackie an "introvertness" and "stiffness" for whom it was "difficult...to show her feelings." Jack and Jackie played out the most intimate personal hardship on the international stage,[232] revealing themselves in ways that heretofore had been unseen, even by each other.

Within ten minutes after Patrick's "tiny white coffin was placed in the ground," the president was aboard Marine I on his way to Jackie. They spent an hour together in her room before Jack once again began hop-scotching back and forth between the kids at Squaw Island and Jackie's bedside.

On Sunday morning he attended the 10:00 a.m. mass at Hyannis's St. Francis Xavier Church. He listened as Pastor Monsignor Leonard Daley offered a prayer. "In our sorrow for them." intoned the monsignor, "we know one consolation is that they have given back to God, their maker, a saint in heaven praying for them through these troubled times."[233]

The next two days, Jack brought the children to see their mom—first Caroline, then John, then the two together. John was playful, bounding up and down the stairs to the helicopter, his ever-present toy helicopter in his hands. Caroline was wistful, sitting on her daddy's lap, gazing out the window at the boats cruising Lewis Bay. Jack turned to the solitude of the sea, taking a half hour on the speed boat *Restuvus* before returning to say goodbye to Jackie on his way back to Washington.

A watershed is defined as a turning point in a course of action or state of affairs. These moments are transformative experiences that occur in the life of a nation and in the lives of its individual citizens. They serve as demarcations in the course of the human experience, after which the citizen, the nation, or both are permanently transformed.

The thirty-nine-hour life of Patrick Bouvier Kennedy transformed the lives of his parents, both as individuals and as a couple. It actually began during Jackie's pregnancy and dramatically intensified on the morning of Patrick's death. After watching their baby boy take his last breath, Jack Kennedy entered Jackie's room and sobbed in her arms. She had "never seen anything like that in him," and she was "stunned" by it.[234] Within the depth of their profound sadness, Jackie found hope—hope for him, hope for herself, and hope for them together.

Clint Hill immediately witnessed "a distinctively closer relationship, openly expressed, between the president and Mrs. Kennedy."[235] The world witnessed it for the first time four days after Patrick's burial.

Jack takes Jackie's hand and leads her from the hospital at Otis Air Force Base, one week after Patrick's birth. Patrick's death brought the two of them closer together, illustrated by this very rare public display of affection.

Marine I was waiting for the president to take his wife home. Scores of press members, on watch for what was now a week, were gathered outside. "There were so many of them, just standing outside the hospital door, like vultures, waiting,"[236] recalled Nancy Tuckerman. Consideration was given to finding a different egress, but Jackie told Pam Turnure, "I can do it."[237] Clad in her pink sundress, forsaking makeup and sunglasses, and with her hand in Jack's, they exited the front door into the Cape Cod sunlight and the vultures' den. He walked her to the vehicle's open rear door, not letting go of her hand until she was secured in the backseat. He then made his way around and slid into the seat next to her.

They boarded Marine I for the flight home. Landed, the chopper blades quieted, and they emerged. She took hold of the railing with her right hand and he with his left. His right arm was around her waist, and together they navigated the six steps to the ground. Leaning on each other, they carefully negotiated one step at a time, she clearly still suffering the effects of her surgery and he clearly guarding his chronically painful back. Reaching the final step, Jack took firm hold of the rail with his left hand, while holding tightly to her waist with his right arm. Leaning on him, she gingerly placed first one, then the other foot on the ground. With Jackie secure, he stepped off and guided her to the front seat of their convertible before making his way to the driver's side. The Secret Service agents followed as Jack drove Jackie home.

Paul "Red" Fay caught a glimpse of the change in Jack and Jackie's relationship days before Patrick's birth. The "Redhead," as he was called by Jack, or "Grand Old Loveable," as he often signed his White House correspondence, was visiting in Hyannis Port. His bride, Anita, and their daughter, Sally, accompanied the president and first lady for a weekend at Brambletyde. Following a cruise on the *Honey Fitz* and a swim in Lewis Bay, it was back to the house to change for a trip to downtown Hyannis with Caroline, John, and Sally. The Redhead went upstairs and knocked on the door to Jack's room.

"Come in," said Jack. Fay opened the door to find Jack and Jackie lying in bed together.

"God almighty," said Fay. "Why did you tell me to come in? I don't want to walk in here." There they were, the expectant couple, "lying there in each other's arms and chatting." As "very embarrassing" as it was for Fay, the president just looked at him and said, "Oh, that's all right."[238]

Another old war buddy and Jack's assistant secretary of the Treasury James Reed noted a heretofore unseen attentiveness one weekend in Hyannis. "President Kennedy was extremely solicitous of Jackie and very careful in making certain that everything was all right." He recalled an incident in which the president came downstairs looking for Jackie's doctor. "He asked if I would try to get hold of Dr. Walsh...So I tried to get him and I could not locate him. He [JFK] was very, very upset." It took nearly an hour before Walsh was located, and he immediately came to the house. Although highly perturbed, the president's admonishment was simply to say, "I just hope that if you do go off for a walk for any period of time that you always tell someone where you are, how you can be reached immediately in case I do have to get in touch with you."[239]

Artist William Walton occupied a unique position in Jack and Jackie's lives. He met Jack in 1947 and then lived in the same Georgetown neighborhood when they were newlyweds, becoming a confidant and friend to both.

Jackie's first week home found Jack returning for a mid-week overnight stay and an early weekend arrival on Friday. The following weekend proved dreary as rain brought more of an early November feel than late August. No doubt the gloomy weather contributed to the mood, and Jackie, now three weeks post-partum, was clearly sinking into depression. It had accompanied previous pregnancies and obviously was exacerbated by the trauma of losing Patrick. Even the attentiveness and concern of her husband could not stem the throes of it.

Walton was their only guest that weekend. "It was just the two of them, the kids and me," Walton told Ralph Martin. "Probably the most intimate weekend I've ever had with them." Saturday marked a very rare occasion, as nobody left the house, the normal activities curtailed by sorrow and the rain. Walton recalled that "the house was full of sadness...We were sitting in his office and...he was going through condolences from the leaders of the world...then we went swimming...and he unburdened himself of everything from Khrushchev to Berlin."[240]

French philosopher and poet Alphonse de Lamartine once wrote, "Grief knits two hearts in closer bonds than happiness ever can, and common sufferings are far stronger links than common joys." Walton clearly observed a transformation. "Jack and Jackie were very close after Patrick's death," he said. "She hung onto him and he held her in his arms."[241]

Touched by his tenderness, Jackie observed, "He never said so, but I know he wanted another boy. John was such a pure joy for him. Most men don't care about children as much as women do, but he did. He felt the loss of the baby in the house as much as I did."[242] The "stronger link" born of "grief" and "common suffering" knitted their hearts, bringing them closer to each other in ways they had never known. It was a closeness best articulated when Jackie said to him, "The one blow I could not bear would be to lose you."[243]

Ted Kennedy recalled that bond in his memoir. "In the few months left to him, my brother showed an even greater preoccupation with the activities of his son and daughter than I had ever seen before. And he was concerned for Jackie...Over these months...Jack's greatest concern was for his wife's and children's welfare."[244]

Jackie remained in Hyannis Port through the revelry of the Kennedy patriarch's seventy-fifth birthday. Then it was off to Hammersmith Farm and their tenth-anniversary weekend, when the Bradlees saw them embrace each other like they had never seen before. The weekend celebration included cruises aboard the *Honey Fitz* and the couples golfing at the Newport Country Club.

The weekend boosted Jackie's spirits, and she decided to travel to Greece with Lee. She returned refreshed with renewed strength enough to make the trip with Jack to Texas.

Jackie put her speech away and returned to the bedroom to change into a white dress with a matching black belt and beret. Mary Gallagher had just finished buttoning up the back when a gentle tap was heard at the door. "You all right?" her husband asked.

"Fine," she said through a radiant smile at his reflection in her mirror. He turned to make his way up the corridor, and the chief steward intercepted him. "We've entered into our glide pattern, Mr. President." [245]

The reception for Jack and Jackie was overwhelming in every city they visited in Texas. It began here in San Antonio and marked Jackie's first trip with Jack since Patrick's death. Jackie's presence doubled the crowds and doubled the enthusiasm.

On the ground, Lyndon Johnson and Texas governor John Connally were in a receiving line awaiting their arrival. Air Force I began its taxi toward the terminal, and a woman cried out, "Jackie!" The crowd quickly picked up the mantra, "Jackie, Jackie, Jackie!" The presidential plane rolled to a stop, the ramp was wheeled into place, the hatch opened, and America's first couple stood in the doorway. Jackie held Jack's arm for a brief second before the president, breaking protocol, stepped back, letting her lead the way. A roar went up from the assembled thousands. After receiving a bouquet of yellow Texas roses, the first lady joined her husband and Governor and Mrs. Connally in the back of a convertible for the first of the day's six motorcades.

The road to Brooks Air Force Base was lined with people throughout the outskirts of the city. Signs were everywhere, including one hand-lettered placard that implored Jackie to come water ski in Texas. Secret Service agents were kept busy as overenthusiastic fans sporadically rushed the limousine to steal a handshake from the president and first lady. One group of youngsters made a charge toward the motorcade and were joined by a half dozen St. Joseph's nuns, all trying to touch the president. Sitting across from him in the backseat, Jackie was beaming.

Approaching downtown, the crowds grew increasingly larger. Little children sat on the curbstones while their parents stood six and eight deep behind them. There was no school in San Antonio, and students were everywhere. Conversation within the vehicle was rendered impossible by the screams of the crowd. William Baily, seventeen at the time, remembered, "It was like a king and queen coming to visit." Although the crowd once again thinned as they left the downtown area, hundreds of people, both young and old, sprinted after the motorcade in the hope of catching a closer look at the "king" and his beaming "queen."[246]

Jackie stood at her husband's side on the platform as the band played "Hail to the Chief," and at the appointed moment they strolled together across the stage. He took his position at the lectern, and she took her seat next to Lyndon Johnson.

President Kennedy's speech reaffirmed his New Frontier. Outlining the perils inherent in space exploration, he emphasized the pioneer spirit required to face its challenges. Chiding the naysayers who claimed it was a waste of time and resources, he offered "that nothing could be further from the truth…the wartime development of radar gave us the transistor and all that it made possible." Listening intently, Jackie thought to herself, "I never knew that."[247] He continued, "Research in space medicine holds the promise of substantial benefit." Our space effort "is not a competitor for natural resources that we need...It is a working partner and co-producer of these resources."

His speech concluded, and General Theodore Bedwell and his command staff escorted the president and first lady on a short walk. Their destination was a review of a space-age experiment. Four volunteers had entered a hyperbaric chamber simulating the pure oxygen environment of a space capsule at twenty-seven thousand feet. Its purpose was to study the long-term effects of that environment on humans. The four young men were eighteen days into a forty-two-day project.

Bedwell led the Kennedys to Dr. Billy Welch, the experiment's project manager. Following a brief introduction, the president took hold of a headset. Philip Jameson, seventeen at the time, recalled the encounter fifty years later. "We were…mingling here [by the window] for a minute or two then all of a sudden we heard 'He's here.'" Looking into the chamber over the president's shoulder, Welch recalled, "I can always remember one thing and that is the look on the guy's face when he heard his voice."

"Heart stopped," said Jameson. "There he was…and I had to take in the whole picture of him for a few seconds to really realize that this was President Kennedy." Inquisitive, Kennedy asked how they were doing and about their goals for the mission. Then he asked about any benefits they could foresee coming from it, to which Jameson replied, "We get to meet you." Before leaving, the president told the men that they were the "perfect models" for his call to "ask not what your country can do for you but what you can do for your country."[248]

Removing the headset, Jack and Jackie engaged in a private conversation with Dr. Welch. They inquired if this data would have applications to medical issues related to newborns. They knew all too well the "promise of substantial benefits" of space medicine research, for the loss of Patrick was still deep in their hearts.

Another motorcade to Kelly Air Force Base and Air Force I brought them to their next stop: Houston. A small row of dignitaries and local police lined their path to boarding. President Kennedy always made a point to shake the hands of local police protection when he departed an area. These San Antonio gendarmes had the additional bonus of a handshake from Jackie as well.

It was five o'clock when Air Force I rolled to a stop at Houston International Airport, and once again it was Jackie leading the way to the University of Houston Marching Band playing the Marine Corps hymn. There were more yellow roses, more welcomes from local dignitaries, and more expressions of well-wishers from a gathered throng. Approximately ten thousand people were at the airport, and true to form, the president headed into the crowd. Jackie followed and was nearly crushed by their enthusiasm. At one point, both her wrists were grasped, and she felt like she would be dragged over the wall. Despite an inner panic she maintained her composure, and her smile never waned.

Nearly 200,000 people lined the streets of downtown Houston as the day's third motorcade snaked toward the Rice Hotel. Forty-five minutes behind schedule, the first couple ate "supper off trays in the room...The Vice President walked in," recalled Pam Turnure, "and everybody seemed in a very buoyant mood...very relaxed and...going well."[249] The Secret Service informed the LULAC gathering that the president and first lady would drop by for a wave but could not attend.

With the presidential limo in waiting, the seven-hundred-plus members of LULAC clustered around the door in the hope of getting a closer look at the "king" and "queen." The first couple came into view, and it was clear that the gathering was about to experience far more than a simple presidential wave.

Once more Jackie was leading the way. Adorned in a black dress and white gloves, she entered the room. Three strings of white pearls hung from her neck. The president followed as the gathering erupted with applause and cheers. Shouts of "Bravo!" could be heard as Jackie made her way to the front of the stage. She shook hands with Fernando Herrera, a musician in the band. "I couldn't believe it, I couldn't believe it," recalled Herrera. "How

The University of Houston Marching Band and 10,000 people greeted them in Houston. Another 200,000 awaited them lining the streets through downtown.

beautiful they were, they glowed, they glowed." Jack and Jackie turned to acknowledge the crowd as the band broke into song. A short reception line was formed as the president and first lady greeted some of the guests. Twenty-eight-year-old Tina Adame shook Jackie's hand and said, "You are more beautiful in person than you are in any photograph." The first lady beamed. "She looked very happy to be here," Adame remembered.[250]

To the glee of all, President Kennedy moved to the podium to speak. His brief address closed with: "In order that my words will be even clearer, I'm going to ask my wife to say a few words to you also." The room sprang to its collective feet, and a roar went up as they applauded Jackie's stroll to the podium. Jack backed off, and as Jackie took center stage, she rested her hands

Jackie spoke in Spanish to the LULAC Convention the evening of November 21. "Once Jackie spoke, you forgot all about the president," said Tina Adame, present that evening. Dave Powers said Jack and Jackie had exchanged eyes, and Lady Bird Johnson said that the president looked beguiled.

on the side of the rostrum. Before speaking she turned around to look at her husband. Their eyes met, and he smiled.

She began in Spanish, saying, "I am very happy to be in the grand state of Texas. And I'm especially happy to be with you who form part of the noble Spanish tradition that has contributed so much to Texas. And this tradition began 100 years before the colonization of Massachusetts, the state my husband comes from. But it's a tradition you have sustained for a long time." Another round of resounding applause was heard, and a man called out, "Viva, Mrs. Kennedy, viva Kennedy!" Jackie concluded, "You are working for Texas and the United States. Thank you very much and long live LULAC." Jack's eyes never left her, and the only thing brighter than his smile was hers. Clint Hill remarked, "You could see in the president's face just how proud he was, how pleased he was."[251] Dave Powers wrote that they had "exchanged eyes,"[252] and Mrs. Johnson thought that the president looked "beguiled."[253]

She walked back to her seat in front of the stage, and Jack followed, applauding and then gently taking her arm as he settled in the chair next to her. "When Jackie spoke, you forgot all about the president," remembered Adame. "It was all about Jackie, and then her speaking in Spanish overshadowed anything he said."[254] And he could not have been happier.

Another ride through Houston's darkened streets took them to the Houston Coliseum and the fundraising dinner for Congressman Albert Thomas. This was the part of politics that Jackie detested—boring politicians bloviating. On the way she asked, "Who organized this testimonial for Albert Thomas anyway?"

"Albert Thomas," came the president's sardonic reply. "He made the plans, wrote speeches praising himself, ran all over the..."

She looked at him. "Jack," she said, bringing his soliloquy to an end.[255]

There were 3,300 patrons in the smoke-filled coliseum, all paying tribute to Thomas. The worst part was that the president and first lady would be seated on opposite sides of the rostrum. The best part was that President Kennedy would deliver a ten- to fifteen-minute speech and they would be on their way. He took the rostrum and immediately won over the crowd with his self-deprecating wit. He poked fun at his own early days in Congress and made light of the names that presidents are sometimes called. He then went full thrust, complimenting Thomas and his leadership role in moving America into space. A slip of the tongue turned out to be the highlight of the evening. Deviating from his prepared address, Kennedy said of Thomas, "He has helped steer this country to its eminence in space...Next month when the United States of America...fires the largest payroll, payload, giving us the lead." Catching his gaffe, the president paused a few seconds and then

Jackie listens to Jack's last speech of the day, November 21 at the Houston Coliseum dinner honoring Texas congressman Albert Thomas. What she would remember about this speech was Jack's quoting from the Book of Acts, "Your young men will see visions, your old men will dream dreams."

said, "It will be the largest payroll, too. And who should know that better than Houston?" The coliseum roared with laughter.

What Jackie would remember from that night was not the laughter but the bible verse Jack quoted in conclusion: "Your old men will dream dreams, your young men will see visions, the bible tells us, and where there is no vision, the people perish. Albert Thomas is old enough to dream dreams and young enough to see visions."[256]

The day's fifth motorcade was to Houston International, where Air Force I was prepared for the forty-five-minute hop to Fort Worth's Carswell Air Force Base. A light rain had begun to fall as Air Force I touched down at 11:07 p.m., yet several thousand residents had gathered to welcome the first couple to "Cowtown." Children waved placards while their parents cheered as Jack and Jackie deplaned for the final time of the day. Weary and fatigued, they made their way to the barriers to greet the throng. Bob Machos, an eight-year-old third grader, was in the crowd with a friend. They were both wearing their school sweaters. The president had walked by and passed them over, but Jackie noticed their sweaters. She called, "Jack, there's some Catholic schoolboys here." She looked down at them, "Do you all go to Catholic school?" Looking up, star struck, the boys answered, "Yes," and the first lady bent down and kissed them both on the head.[257] The president came back and followed up his lady's kiss with a pat before moving on down the line.

They entered a black Cadillac limousine for their final ride of the day. Riding with them was *Houston Chronicle* publisher John Jones and his wife Freddie. Jack and Jones talked politics while Freddie told Jackie about the city. She liked Fort Worth, "a small poor town…proud of being known as Cowtown." She did not speak highly, however, of Dallas. "It's a merchant's town…really a terrible town." As the last ride of the day came to an end, Jackie wondered what Dallas would be like.[258]

A light show normally reserved for holidays welcomed them downtown. Clint Hill recalled, "The city wanted to put on a show for President and Mrs. Kennedy and they did."[259] The buildings in downtown Fort Worth were artistically illuminated, creating the look of a fantasyland.

It was near midnight when they entered the Texas Hotel under the blazing marquee that read, "WELCOME MR. PRESIDENT." Their long day's journey into night finally had come to an end. Seventeen hours had passed since the dawning of their day in the nation's capital, a day that consisted of six motorcades, three plane rides, speeches, thousands of handshakes, and one continuous smile. "From the moment she stepped out of the blue nosed presidential jet in San Antonio…Mrs. Kennedy lit up the state like a gusher on fire. The eyes of Texas are for her, overwhelmingly." When it was over Jackie remarked, it was "a happy day," and "she looked as if she had enjoyed every minute."[260]

They were sitting in his room together. "You were great today," he said to her. "How do you feel?"

"Oh gosh," came her reply, "I'm exhausted." He was half asleep, and he called to her as she was leaving, "Don't get up with me. I've got to speak in that square before breakfast, but stay in bed. Just be downstairs for breakfast at 9:15."[261]

Jackie had never felt closer to him, and the passion of the day moved into the night. Secretary Mary Gallagher had gone, lost in the shuffle of planes and automobiles, so Jackie had to lay out her clothes for the next day: "navy blue blouse, navy handbag, low-heeled shoes, pink suit and pill box hat."[262] Then she returned to Jack's room and "slipped into her husband's bed… aroused him from his exhaustion and they made love for the last time."[263]

Friday's Fort Worth Chamber of Commerce breakfast was scheduled for 8:45 a.m., and they would leave the hotel at 10:30 a.m. for the motorcade to Carswell Air Force Base. The twenty-minute flight to Dallas's Love Field was to take off at 11:15 a.m.

A light but steady rain fell throughout most of the night, but it did not stop five coeds from Amon Carter High School. The first to assemble, it was 5:00 a.m. when they took up their positions. The Secret Service was already in place, their rifled observers perched on rooftops. It was not long before agents came down and spoke to them. "We'll make sure when he comes down...we will...guide him over to you," they told them, "and you'll get to have an up close look at him and shake his hand and meet him."[264]

Upstairs the president was dressing when he moved through Jackie's room to take a peek at the street eight stories below. "Look at the crowd," he exclaimed. "Just look," he repeated. "Isn't it terrific?" Immediately energized, he scooted back to his room to finish dressing. Scarfing down a breakfast of coffee and half a roll, he was knotting his tie when Dave Powers entered.

"Have you seen the square?" he enthusiastically inquired. "And weren't the crowds great in San Antonio and Houston?" Powers nodded as Jack added, "And you were right...They loved Jackie."[265] The adulation of Jackie by Thursday's throngs in San Antonio, Houston, and Fort Worth was not lost on the White House Press Corps. On the political front, the focus of coverage was on the rift in the Democratic party of Texas. However, on the campaigning front, the story was Jackie, Jackie, and more Jackie.

The *Austin Statesman* splashed the headlines, "Jackie Shines" amidst four Jackie photos. "Radiant First Lady Charms Houston," read the *Baytown Sun*, and in Amarillo, the *Globe Times* announced, "Jackie Draws Texas Cheers." The *Corpus Christi Caller* proclaimed, "Jackie Big Hit," and even the *Dallas Morning News* acknowledged that Jackie "Brings Down the House in Houston." The *Chicago Sun-Times* summed up Jackie's political impact, noting, "Some Texans, in taking account of the tangled Texas political situation, have begun to think that Mrs. Jacqueline Kennedy may turn the balance and win her husband this state's electoral votes."[266]

Larry O'Brien entered. The president was looking out the window, watching as workers put some finishing touches on the podium from where he would soon speak. O'Brien joined him at the window. Always fatalistic about his vulnerability, the president said, "You know when they talk about security and protecting you…look at this, if somebody wants to get you, they can always do it."[267]

At 8:45 a.m., President Kennedy walked out of the front entrance of the hotel and, to their delight, walked directly to the coed girls. He began to work the crowd in the inimitable JFK fashion, and the first thing he heard was: "Where's Jackie?" Smiling he responded, "You know how ladies are, they have to have their beauty rest."

Jackie Kennedy's day dawned with a new hope, a hope filled with life. For the first time since the birth and death of Patrick, the flow of life moved through her. She and Jack wanted more children, but Jackie was

Jack arose early to give a speech in the parking lot on November 22 in Fort Worth. He was greeted with shouts, "Where's Jackie?" Jack turned and pointed up to the eighth floor saying, "Mrs. Kennedy is organizing herself, it takes longer but of course she looks better than we do."

apprehensive and worried it would never happen. She now knew it could and knowing that the possibility again existed filled her with joy. It was a joy that could only spring from hope.[268]

The president worked his way across the front of the line and then took the podium. "There are no faint hearts in Fort Worth," he began when a voice came from the crowd, "Where's Jackie?" He paused. "Mrs. Kennedy is organizing herself, it takes longer but of course she looks better than we do when she does it." Sitting above the crowd, on his father's shoulders, was eight-year-old Bill Paxton. "Seeing him so alive, and not in black and white but in person, his red hair, bigger than life, there was this joyous excitement in the air, this wasn't just a president, this was President Kennedy."[269]

He spoke but a minute and a half, concluding with: "Here in this rain, in Fort Worth, in Texas we're moving forward." And he returned to the crowd, which was sprinkled with about one thousand young ladies sporting newly coiffed "Jackie Dos." Calls of "Mr. President, Mr. President" were heard pleading for a handshake. "Thank you, thank you," he repeated, making his way along the line, and he came upon seventeen-year-old Kay Fredericks, one of the five Amon Carter coeds he had initially greeted. "I've already shaken your hand haven't I," he said to her. "Yes, Mr. President," she said with a smile, "and with that he turned around and walked inside." His final speech awaited.[270]

First it was back upstairs to change his suit, now spotted by the rain, causing a twenty-minute delay while the more than two thousand members of Fort Worth's Chamber of Commerce waited with great anticipation. Ironically, the vast majority of the folks were Republicans, and according to Cornelia Friedman, the wife of Fort Worth's mayor, "not many of them had even voted for Kennedy."[271] However, it was a palpable, exciting energy moving through that room awaiting not only the president, but the first lady as well.

Vice-President Lyndon Johnson burst through the kitchen door, leading the Texas contingent to the head table. With all eyes glued on the kitchen door, the Eastern Hills High School band struck up "Hail to the Chief," and the president appeared to a roar that drowned out the band. KTVT cameraman Phil Crow remembered, "It was like a Hollywood Star entered the room." However, his initial reaction was surprise that "he was alone."[272] Crow, on the other hand, was not alone. The first words out of news director Ed Herbert's mouth were: "Mrs. Kennedy did not enter with the president and we have no indication of where she may be...And quite a few ladies appear quite disappointed." The disappointment was not reserved to just the "ladies," as Jackie's absence became the focal point of the coverage.

The president was seated, perusing his speech and making notes. Chamber of Commerce president Raymond Buck introduced the Texas Boys Choir, who serenaded the president with the "Eyes of Texas Are Upon You." However, all eyes were upon the empty seat between the president and vice-president. The empty seat was now the story. "We have been watching the head table closely," said Herbert, "and so far there's been no coffee placed at Mrs. Kennedy's spot at the table, and no breakfast has been set down. This indicates she will not appear." He began a virtual play-by-play of the maître d's movements. "Again he's pouring coffee as he's moving down the line and again he did not stop in Mrs. Kennedy's place."[273]

Upstairs in suite 850, Clint Hill was with the first lady. In his pocket was a copy of Mrs. Kennedy's schedule in which she had made a notation next to the morning breakfast that read, "JBK will not attend." The phone rang. "Clint...the president wants you to bring Mrs. Kennedy down right now."[274]

"But Mrs. Kennedy isn't intending on going to the breakfast," came Hill's reply. Hill learned that was no longer an option and that, in fact, "the president wants her down here now."

Raymond Buck was stalling for time, informed by the president that Mrs. Kennedy was "on her way." Word raced throughout the room, finally making its way to the television audience and bringing applause and a buzz of anticipation to the crowded ballroom. Buck returned to the podium and again called upon another number from the Boys Choir. In his folksy Texas manner, he took nearly ten minutes introducing the nine head table guests and their wives, closing with "Mr. O.C. Yancy, president of the Central Trade Council." The applause softened and then ceased.

An anticipating silence came over the room, with all eyes now turned toward the kitchen point of entry. A gentleman came behind Buck and whispered to him. "All right, all right," said Buck, and he leaned to the microphone. "And now, here is an event I know all of you have been waiting for." Applause instantaneously erupted, and a cheer went up as the room sprang to its collective feet. Jackie Kennedy walked in.[275] Many of the guests stood on their chairs to get a better look at the first lady. Radiant and beaming in her

Jackie is led by Clint Hill to the head table in the grand ballroom at Fort Worth's Texas Hotel. Jackie originally opted out of the breakfast but the crowd simply would not allow it. Cornelia Friedman, wife of Fort Worth's mayor, said she looked like a "mythical figure."

ensemble, which she had laid out the night before, she dazzled and delighted the gathering. "When Jackie…walked in she captivated everyone," [276] recalled attendee Roy McDurmutt. She made her way through the crowd to the accompaniment of accolades: "Oh isn't she lovely?" "My, she's even prettier in person," and "Look at that stunning suit." [277] Standing and clapping, leading the welcome, was her husband. He, too, was beaming. Cornelia Friedman was sitting five seats to the left of Jackie at the head table. "She looked like something out of a mythological story and he was standing there looking like the All American boy." [278]

Jackie took her seat, and Buck returned to the podium. "He has honored us with his presence and that of the charming and lovely first lady," he began. "May God bless you and cause his light to shine on you and on your companions and your family," Buck intoned. And then, "Ladies and gentleman I proudly present the President of the United States." [279] Another eruption of applause and cheers followed, and then Jack Kennedy did what he did best. With his trademark, self-deprecating wit, he took over the room.

In her first interview with Arthur Schlesinger, Jackie commented on how she was struck by how many different types of people "think that Jack is theirs. You'd think he belonged to so many people," she said, "and each one thought they had him completely."

The reality was that he had them completely, and it was no different in the grand ballroom of Fort Worth's Texas Hotel on the morning of November 22, 1963. Referencing Buck's head table introductions, he complimented the throng. "I know now why everyone in Texas, Fort Worth is so thin. Having gotten up and down about nine times. This is what you do every morning." Also fully aware of the true star of the day, he acknowledged his wife and, in his perfect cadence, punctuating thoughts with his patented ah, he said, "Two years ago I said that, ah, I introduced myself in Paris by saying that I was the man who had accompanied, ah, Mrs. Kennedy to Paris. I'm getting somewhat that same sensation, ah, as I travel around, ah, Texas." The crowd cheered, and then he brought the house down. "Nobody wonders what Lyndon and I wear," and when the uproarious laughter subsided he began his speech.

He spoke for about twelve minutes, highlighting Fort Worth's contributions to the defense of the United States. He concluded, "I'm confident, as I look to the future that our chances for security, our chances for peace, are better than they've been in the past. And the reason is because we're stronger. And with that strength is a determination to not only maintain the peace but also the vital interests of the United States. To that great cause Texas and the United States are committed. Thank you."

The crowd erupted into cheers and were once again on their feet. Jackie was leading the way, looking down on her husband, who had taken his seat. The raucous clapping and cheering went on until the president rose to acknowledge them. It was Jackie who now looked beguiled. Buck resumed the podium to present gifts to the first couple. Scheduled to close out the trip with a visit to the LBJ Ranch on the weekend, Buck presented each with a pair of boots for protection against the rattlesnakes. They also gave the president a ten-gallon Texas cowboy hat, which the crowd implored him to put on. In what would become a most poignant moment in history, the president returned to the dais, broadly smiling. "I'll put it on in the White House on Monday," he told them. "If you come up there you'll have a chance to see it then." Watching him dodge donning the cowboy hat, Jackie thought of Lady Bird's inquiry about what the president might want to do at the ranch. "I'd like to ride," he told her, and her mind wandered to Newport, Rhode Island, ten years ago, when they galloped bareback through the fields. She thought of how handsome he'd look riding under that Stetson.[280]

An invocation followed, and then Jack and Jackie made their way through the back side of the head table. The other guests formed a makeshift receiving line, and the president and first lady shook every hand on their way back to the kitchen doorway, which would now serve as an exit. Cornelia Freedman was in the line. "We quite frankly I don't think had voted for

Kennedy, but I will say by the end of the day, just like everybody else, we were totally captivated."[281] True to form, the first couple broke ranks and for a few brief moments surged into the crowd to greet them and shake hands, Jackie working one side while the president worked the other.

A grueling day awaited that included seven motorcades. The first would take forty-five minutes back to Carswell followed by a flight to Dallas's Love Field. The last would take them from the Municipal Auditorium in Austin to Bergstrom Air Force Base for a chopper to the LBJ Ranch, arriving somewhere near midnight. However, they now had an hour respite, and they returned to suite 850.

Jackie was lighthearted and cheerful, energized by both the reception she'd received and the news that they had an hour to relax. "Oh Jack," she said upon hearing that news, "campaigning is so easy when you're president...I'll go anywhere with you this year."

The president laughed, "How about California the next two weeks?"

"I'll be there," came her quick reply.

He turned to Ken O'Donnell, who had just walked in the room. "Did you hear that?"[282]

Jackie's reply brought a rare smile to O'Donnell's seemingly terminally stone face; in fact, he remembered "grinning like an ape."[283]

Jack placed a phone call, and while he was talking, Jackie, for the first time, noticed the art work adorning the walls of their suite. The drab walls had been transformed into a gallery of priceless art, and the first lady was quite taken by it. She perused the catalogue, explaining the treasures that surrounded them—treasures that had been arranged in their honor.

The president hung up the phone, and Jackie showed him the catalogue. "Isn't this sweet, Jack?" she said. "They've just stripped their whole museum of all their treasures to brighten this dingy hotel suite." Knowing that this had been done for her benefit, Jack said, "Let's see who did it," and she turned to the end of the catalogue.[284]

Jack and Jackie had no idea what had transpired to bring the likes of Picasso, Van Gogh, Claude Monet, and others to their "dingy" suite on what would be their last night together. Sadly, like all the other events of San Antonio, Houston, and Fort Worth, it became but a footnote to the tragedy of Dallas.

It all began with a front-page story in the *Fort Worth Press* on Sunday, November 17, four days before the scheduled arrival of the president and Mrs. Kennedy. Under the headline "Suite Eight-Fifty…It'll Be Famous," staff writer Jean Wysatta detailed the three room suite. A half century later, Fort Worth art historian Scott Grant Barker encapsulated it thusly: "Vaguely Chinese furnished…Dutch blue walls that had accents of jade, green and gold, and the art on the walls was just terrible, it was just awful." The "awfulness" mobilized the horrified art community of Fort Worth, primarily Ruth Carter Johnson and Sam Canty.

A sixteen-piece art exhibit was put together on "a handshake and a phone call," resulting in an international art display for the president and first lady. Its installation was completed only hours before the Kennedys' arrival. The impromptu nature of its creation was vividly illustrated by Ruth Carter Johnson's delivery of Picasso's *Angry Owl* sculpture in the front seat of her car, buckled in a seat belt.

Ruth Carter Johnson neither supported John F. Kennedy politically nor had she voted for him. None of that mattered at all when Canty called to ask her to help "bring the museum to the Kennedys." [285]

Both Canty and Johnson understood the impact Jacqueline Kennedy had on popular American culture. They were aware that she had studied in France and that she was multi-lingual. They were among the sixty-seven million Americans who had watched her televised tour of the White House, whose restoration and refurbishing she was overseeing. All of this coupled with her immense support of the arts, music, and poetry led them to one conclusion: "If an Art Exhibit for the President and Mrs. Kennedy was going to please anyone, they wanted it to be her." [286]

The Kennedys found Johnson's name at the top of the catalogue's back-page list. Home caring for a sick child, she was unable to attend the breakfast; she did, however, watch it on television. Sometime around 10:20 a.m. her phone rang. "Mrs. Johnson," the voice said.

"Yes," she replied.

"Please hold for the president."

On the other end of the phone the president of the United States was apologizing to her for not calling the night before, explaining they had not arrived until near midnight. He handed the phone to Mrs. Kennedy, and in what Carter described as a voice sounding "thrilled and vivacious," Jackie said, "They're going to have a dreadful time getting me out of here with all these wonderful works of art. It is too beautiful to let it go so quickly... We're both touched...Thank you so much."[287] They said their goodbyes, and Ruth went about her morning buoyant in spirit at having accomplished her mission. Jackie Kennedy was indeed pleased, very pleased.

The sweetness of the moment was broken when Ken O'Donnell handed the president the *Dallas Morning News* opened to two full-page ads excoriating President Kennedy and his policies. On one side, under mock mug shots of President Kennedy, were the words "WANTED FOR TREASON" with seven "crimes" listed. The other side listed twelve questions that "demanded" answers. Jack read it and handed it to Jackie. "We're heading into nut country," he said, and as Jackie's eyes drank in the ad, her ebullience waned and she felt sick.

Questioning the journalistic integrity of such an ad, the president paced the room and then turned to O'Donnell. "Can you imagine a paper doing a thing like that?" he asked, and then he stopped in front of Jackie. He spoke casually. "You know last night would have been a helluva night to assassinate a president," he said. "I mean it, there was the rain, the night and we were all getting jostled. Suppose a man had a pistol in a briefcase." He then pointed his finger at the wall, turning it into a pistol, and pulled the trigger twice.

He finished, "He could have dropped the gun, and the briefcase and melted away in the crowd."[288]

"Jackie" he added, "if somebody wants to shoot me from a window with a rifle, nobody could stop it, so why worry about it?"[289] She knew him, she knew his coping mechanisms, and through ten years of marriage they had endured their own measure of adversity. He took it lightly, enabling her to shake it off.

Jack and Jackie left the Texas Hotel, and just as he had done all day Thursday, the president walked behind his first lady. Governor John Connally was in the backseat of the Lincoln convertible on loan from a local dealer. He rose as Jackie took her seat, and the president followed. The first of the day's seven scheduled motorcades was underway. The morning rain was gone, and the sun was shining brilliantly. So was Jackie.

This motorcade was no different than the previous days. The cheering multitudes lined Main Street and beyond as the Castleberry High marching band played. Clint Hill recalled, "The crowds were extremely large," and Linda Claridge was delighted that the rain had lifted, which meant the top would be down. "Kennedy weather," Kenny O'Donnell called it. Claridge remembered, "The top was down, the president was kinda leaning out and Mrs. Kennedy looked beautiful...Chanel pink, with the navy blue, she was just beautiful."[290]

Arriving at Carswell, they immediately walked to the line of waiting people and began shaking hands. Ten-year-old Rick Irving remembered how "warm" the president's hand was, while his six-year-old brother, Ken, remembered her "small hand, her white glove."[291] The first couple continued down the line, and Jackie reached into the crowd, taking a pen and paper from one lucky spectator and signing her name. Right beside her, an unknown middle-aged woman, wearing a scarf around her head, handed the president a piece of paper, and as Jackie turned and watched, her husband signed his name. They turned away, and Jack reached for Jackie's hand. For a few brief seconds, they walked hand in hand to the line of dignitaries, with most of whom they had shared breakfast. "I was shaking Kennedy's hand," said Cornelia Friedman. "I was very impressed by him and he looked at me and he said, 'I admired your earrings this morning.' At that point I nearly fainted. It was pretty amazing that he noticed my earrings."[292] She watched as the president followed Jackie up the stairs to board Air Force I. Reaching the top they both turned and waved. Smiling broadly, they disappeared inside for the thirteen-minute flight to Dallas. Friedman turned to her husband and said, "I hope they behave themselves in Dallas."[293]

Presidential advance man John Byrne remained in Fort Worth. "I remember everyone coming up to me face(s) glowing...completely

Jack and Jackie, hand in hand, leave the crowd in Fort Worth to board Air Force I for Dallas. The rigorous day of campaigning brought them closer. Jackie had commented earlier in the morning, "campaigning is so easy when you're president...I'll go anywhere with you this year."

delighted...this Texas trip is now really hitting on all cylinders. The reception of the president was very good and for his wife enthusiastic."[294]

On the short hop to Dallas, the Texas rift showed signs of being bridged. Senator Ralph Yarborough had agreed to ride with Vice-President Johnson in the motorcade and Kenny O'Donnell informed the president that Governor Connally had capitulated and Yarborough would sit at the head table for the evening's dinner in Austin. "Terrific," said the president through a grin. "That makes the whole trip worthwhile."[295]

Connally was astonished by the turnouts for Kennedy, and the overall consensus was Jackie's presence doubled the size of virtually every crowd. It was estimated that one million Texans (10 percent of the population) would lay their eyes on the first couple, all lending credence to the assessment of the *Chicago Sun-Times*: "Mrs. Jacqueline Kennedy may turn the balance and win her husband this state's electoral votes."

The vice-president's plane landed first at Love Field to get the president's "welcoming party" in place. They stood waiting for the door to open, and Dave Powers looked them over. "You two look like Mr. and Mrs. America,"[296] he observed, and the rear door of the plane swung open. Jackie appeared to a tumultuous roar of the crowd. Behind her the president cut the air with a half salute, half wave, as they made their way down the stairs. Applause and whistles accompanied the cheers, and at the foot of the stairs Lyndon Johnson was waiting for Jackie. He shrugged, and they both laughed as he greeted her, again, before introducing her to Dallas mayor Earle Cabell. "Dearie" Cabell presented Jackie with a bouquet of red roses. Greetings complete, Jack and Jackie made their way to the fence to greet and shake hands with Dallas's common folk. For a full five minutes, they worked the fence before making their way back to the limousine. "The reception at Love Field had astonished everybody," remembered Sixth Floor Museum curator Gary Mack. "There were no inappropriate signs or gestures or events or anything." To many, if not most, it seemed that John F. Kennedy was, indeed, "the man who had accompanied Mrs. Kennedy to Texas." The enthusiasm was palpable.

Governor Connally, replete with his cowboy hat, was standing in the vehicle. He and his wife, Nellie, were waiting to accompany the Kennedys on their second motorcade of the day. Dave Powers reappeared with a couple of reminders for "Mr. and Mrs. America." "Lunchtime," he said to the president, "we're going to hit that captive audience again." Then he turned to Jackie, "Be sure to look to your left, away from the president, wave to the

Throughout the Texas trip presidential protocol was eschewed as Jackie, to the delight of the gathered throngs, was always the first one to deplane. Here she leads Jack down the ramp to the tarmac of Love Field in Dallas.

people on your side. If you both wave to the same voter, it's a waste."[297] It was 11:55 a.m., Texas time, when the motorcade departed Love Field for the scheduled 12:30 p.m. luncheon at the Dallas Trade Mart. The sky was brilliant, the weather was brilliant, and Jackie Kennedy was radiant.

Snaking through the outskirts of Love Field towards downtown, the crowds were thin. On Lemmon Avenue a group of children stood behind a sign that read, "MR PRESIDENT, PLEASE STOP AND SHAKE OUR HANDS." "Let's stop here, Bill," the president said to driver William Greer,

Jackie shaking hands with some of the very happy crowd along the fence at Dallas's Love Field. Close behind, in sunglasses, is Secret Service agent Clint Hill.

and they were nearly overrun by the horde of youngsters squealing with excitement. Their sign had worked.

The crowds grew commensurate with the motorcade's proximity to downtown, and they grew louder, screaming, "Jack, Jackie!" Nellie Connally recalled, "They seemed to want her as much as they wanted him."[298] Every wave of Jackie's hand brought a collective voice moving like a wave across the crowd. "Jackiiee, Jackiiee, Jackiee!" they shrieked with unabated joy. Across the street, on the president's side of the car, they, too, pleaded with the first lady: "Jackie, Jackie, over here, Jackiiee, over here."[299] They clamored for a look, a wave, a smile. Outside the Holy Trinity Catholic Church, Father Oscar Huber stood with a group of teens from his parish. "Don't kid me," he said to the boys. "You don't care about him, it's Jackie you want to see."[300t]

Jack and Jackie get situated in the back seat of the presidential limousine as they prepare to depart for the motorcade through downtown Dallas and their scheduled luncheon at the Dallas Trade Mart. Just before they departed aide Dave Powers reminded them not to wave to the same voter.

On Main Street the crowds were ten, fifteen and twenty deep. Bill Greer repeatedly moved the vehicle to the left side of the road, keeping the crowd as far away from the president as possible. Four or five times, Clint Hill jumped on the left rear running board, protecting Mrs. Kennedy from the surge. It was a rapturous crowd. Connally remembered it as "huge, warm and enthusiastic...tremendous in size and warmth for the president and first lady.[301] Congressman Jim Wright of Fort Worth was "overjoyed by the marvelously hospitable turnout of the people all the way from Love Field, all the way in through the city, through the city streets." Dallas was "wonderful, gracious and warm," he recalled forty-three years later, with a heartache still creeping into his voice.[302]

The president's car turned right onto Houston Street, leaving the jubilant throngs behind. The unbridled exhilaration and effusiveness of the people of Dallas had incredibly and unexpectedly surpassed the crowds in San Antonio, Houston, and Fort Worth. The acrimonious tone that had accompanied the Dallas visit of Kennedy's UN ambassador Adlai Stevenson one month earlier was nowhere to be seen. "We could see no sign of hostility," wrote Kenny O'Donnell, "not even cool unfriendliness, and the throngs of people jamming the streets and hanging out of windows were all smiling, waving, and shouting excitedly. The steady roar of their cheering was deafening. It was by far the greatest and most emotionally happy crowd we had ever seen in Texas."[303] The frigid anticipated reception melted in November's Texas sun, in the glow of the smiles of President and Mrs. Kennedy, and in the exuberant warmth and affection of the people of Dallas.

Ahead was the Texas School Book Depository, a reddish, sandy-colored brick building. "We will soon be there," said Nellie Connally, and Jackie looked across the plaza toward the triple underpass. "I remember thinking it would be so cool under that tunnel."[304]

Standing with her mother on the corner of Houston and Elm, across the street from the Texas School Book Depository, was eleven-year-old Toni

Glover. "I was fascinated with the Kennedys," she remembered. As the motorcade turned on to Houston, the crowd virtually disappeared, and for an ever-so-brief moment Jack and Jackie turned toward each other. "They spoke to each other," Glover recalled. "They had a couple moment...it made me smile." As the motorcade rolled toward her, covering the two hundred feet of Houston Street, she remembered thinking, "This is the greatest moment of my life." [305]

"There were very few people in that area," recalled Clint Hill, and seeing that, he jumped off the running board behind Mrs. Kennedy and returned to the Secret Service follow-up vehicle. Glancing up at the Book Depository, he noticed "some of the windows were open...but I didn't see anything in those windows." Windows were open along the entire parade route. "People were on balconies, on rooftops, hanging out...of windows." [306]

Sitting in the jump seats of the Secret Service car were Powers and O'Donnell. The president was visibly "thrilled" and "fascinated" by the unexpected reception, and it was clear to both veteran political observers that "the first lady was going to be increasingly valuable in the months ahead." [307]

"This is one state we're going to carry easily," [308] said Kenny O'Donnell.

"We turned there at the courthouse," said Jim Wright. "We were in such a good mood."

Approaching the Book Depository, Nellie Connally, gleeful at the response of the citizens of Dallas, turned to President Kennedy. "You certainly can't say Dallas doesn't love you, Mr. President."

The president smiled, "No, no you can't."

The car was now directly below the ominous building, nearly reaching a complete stop to make the left-hand turn. The triple underpass and freeway entrance were thirty seconds away. "What do you have for time?" O'Donnell asked Powers.

"Twelve-thirty," came the reply. "Not bad…we're only five minutes late."[309]

"I was scanning the left side of the street," said Clint Hill, "and I heard an explosive noise to my right rear. So I scanned from my left to my right going toward that noise…I scanned across the back of the car…I saw the president grabbing his throat."[310]

Jim Wright recalled the irreconcilability of the moment. "I heard the first shot, it sounded like a rifle shot but I couldn't imagine, it was so incongruous to me, the idea that there would be a rifle shot."[311] Governor Connally was seated in front of the president. "I heard this shot...I immediately thought it was a rifle shot."[312] Connally and Wright were hunters, but the sound of rifle shots was foreign to the first lady.

"There is always noise in a motorcade," recalled Jackie Kennedy. "And there are always motorcycles around us…backfiring." The vehicle was halfway down Elm Street, and the shade she had been longing for was less than two hundred feet away. "I was looking to the left…there was a noise… It didn't seem like any different noise really. But then Governor Connally was yelling 'Oh no, no, no.'"

Clint Hill jumped from the running board of the follow-up car and sprinted toward the Lincoln. Jackie was wondering, "Why is he [Connally] screaming?" and then she turned toward her husband. "He had this sort of quizzical look on his face…he never made a sound." Clearly seeing he was in distress, she reached for him, raising her right arm and leaning toward him, when another loud reverberating explosion pierced the plaza. "I could see a piece of his skull, sort of wedge shaped…it was flesh colored with little ridges at the top…he just looked as if he had a slight headache. And I just remember seeing that. No blood or anything."[313]

"Just before I got to the car," said Hill, "there was a third shot, and it hit the president in the head…causing an explosion…brain matter and blood, bone fragments splattered...they came all over the car, me and Mrs. Kennedy."[314] Hill reached the car as Mrs. Kennedy was climbing on the back of the trunk in an attempt to retrieve portions of her husband's shattered skull. Nearly felled by Greer's quick acceleration, a final lunge enabled him to board the trunk and get Jackie back into the car. Just as he did, the president's lifeless body fell onto her lap, and his blood poured from the cavernous head wound. What was not absorbed by her pink suit poured onto the seat, the roses, and the floor.

Hill now covered the first lady, who was cradling her husband's splintered, broken head. "Get to a hospital!" he screamed, and Bill Greer slammed his foot on the gas towards the Stemmons Freeway. Jackie was now shouting, "Oh my God, they've killed my husband! Jack, Jack, I love you Jack." The car reached speeds of eighty miles per hour, with Jackie holding on to her husband, "trying to hold his hair on and his skull on," all the while repeating, "They've killed my husband. I have his brains in my hands."[315]

The one blow she could not bear was now hers to endure. Jack was lost. And through tears, fifty years later, Toni Glover recalled, "For me it was the death of hope."[316]

It took four minutes to reach Parkland Memorial Hospital, but it felt like an eternity to Jackie Kennedy. Winston Lawson and another man dashed into the hospital and retrieved two gurneys for the leaders who lay bleeding in the car. The governor had to be removed first to gain access to the president. Jackie hovered over Jack, cradling his mutilated head and holding it to her breast.

Dave Powers, ignoring shouts from Emory Roberts to stop, bounded out of the vehicle and rushed toward his wounded friend, his mind rejecting what his eyes had already seen. "It couldn't be, it couldn't be," he thought to himself. Jerking open the right rear door, he found the fixed eyes of his dead friend, and his mind could no longer deny the grisly truth. "Oh my God, Mr. President, what have they done to you?" he uttered and burst into tears.[317]

Vehicles streamed into the emergency area, coming to an abrupt halt and unloading. Each arrival added growing numbers of spectators to the ghastly nightmare. Connally was extricated from the middle seat and bound for trauma room two. It was time to move the president. Jackie was not budging. She was clutching him now, and men from the emptying vehicles were gathering around her. The adoring throngs of only minutes before were replaced by panic-stricken, horrified men of power, rendered powerless by what was now her personal horror. She was softly weeping and hugging her husband, unwilling to relinquish her grasp on the last time she would hold him.

Clint Hill leaned over her. "Mrs. Kennedy," he said, "please let us help the president." She didn't move. "Please, we must get the president to a doctor."

"I'm not going to let him go, Mr. Hill," she said without looking up.

"We've got to take him in, Mrs. Kennedy."[318] He placed a hand on her shoulder, unleashing a torrent of anguish, and her shoulders now shook with the heaves of a broken heart. Inaudibly she mumbled, "No, Mr. Hill, you know he's dead. Let me alone."[319]

She lifted her head and looked at him through eyes that reflected her wretched torment, and then he understood. He peeled off his sport jacket and handed it to her. She delicately wrapped her husband's head in Hill's coat. And then she let him go.

Powers, Kellerman, Hill, Lawson, and Greer struggled with the president's 173-pound frame just as Ralph Yarborough came upon the scene. He watched aghast at the disturbing sight of five men trying to get the president's limp body under control. Finally placing him on the gurney, they raced through Parkland's double doors. Jackie raced with them, holding Clint Hill's jacket in place, protecting her husband's privacy and his dignity, an unknown first step in protecting and preserving his legacy. Eight minutes had passed since rifle shots echoed across Dealey Plaza, and John F. Kennedy, case 24740 white male, gunshot wound, was wheeled into Parkland Hospital's trauma room one. Dave Powers scrawled out three lines on his notepad: "I carried my president on stretcher, ran to emergency room #1, Jackie ran beside stretcher holding on." [320]

Outside in Parkland's parking lot, Congressman Jim Wright wandered around, stupefied. He had seen the remnants of carnage in the presidential limousine, roses smattered with fragments of brain tissue, blood pooled on the seat and floor. And he wondered how the morning could begin with such "ebullient joy" and end with "unutterable pathos" and "unspeakable sadness." [321]

Back in Fort Worth, a pounding on the door of his room aroused advance man John Byrne from a nap. Startled, he heard a voice hollering, "Turn on your radio, your boss is dead." Flipping on the radio, the nightmare was confirmed. "This shattering news just ended everything...Everything was so bright one minute and so dark the next." [322]

The gurney burst into the emergency room, bringing with it the dying chief executive, the mayhem of the streets, and the chaos of the parking lot. They entered trauma room one, which was rapidly filling with bodies. Banging noises echoed throughout the halls and were accompanied by uncharacteristic yelling and screaming through the intercom.

Upstairs in the dining room, Dr. Marion Jenkins, Parkland's chief anesthesiologist, was sitting with colleagues when the loudspeaker pleaded for Dr. Tom Shire, who was out of town. Dr. Robert Jones went to the phone to answer for Shire, returning with the news that "the president's been shot and they're bringing him here." Running across the dining room and down a flight of stairs, Jenkins entered the room to find Dr. James Carrico removing a breathing tube from the president's mouth. Taking his position behind the president's head, he assessed his condition. "He was cyanotic, his face was blue...his pupils were wildly dilated...he had a gasping type respiration... giving a chin jerk. He wasn't dead. His EKG had a dying heart pattern." Dr.

Malcolm Perry entered and immediately began a tracheostomy procedure, providing a breathing apparatus through a surgical opening in the throat. Perry asked for a stool to stand on and gain leverage to apply external heart massage. Application of oxygen improved his EKG. Yet with each chest compression, blood gushed from the head wound, spilling all over Jenkins's pants and into his shoes. It had been approximately fifteen minutes since Jackie heard Governor Connally yelling, "Oh, no, no, no."

The intensity of the maniacal freneticism that marked that infinitesimal block of time left Jackie numb and dazed. In the midst of the pandemonium surrounding her, she stood alone. Lady Bird Johnson wrote in her diary, "She was quite alone. I don't think I ever saw anyone so much alone in my life." The wheels of government descended upon a tiny county hospital, and as hysteria, panic, and discord swirled about her, Jackie stood, an island of solitude born of a shattered soul.

Jackie was circling through the trauma room to be guided back out by a variety of individuals. Jenkins recalled, "She was wide eyed, looked at a fifty yard stare, she didn't see anything it appeared. [She was] white, drawn in the face, looking very remote, shocked." The first two or three times she came through the room, Jackie was holding her hands in a cupped position, her left hand over her right. "She came and nudged me with her elbow...and she handed me what was in her right hand...a big chunk of the president's brain."[323]

Father Oscar Huber who, ninety minutes before, had cheered the first couple on the motorcade route, was now standing in the room. Jenkins, knowing Huber's purpose but not fully understanding the Roman Catholic concept of Extreme Unction, approached the priest. "What's the proper time to declare one dead?" he asked, ascertaining how the declaration of death would impact Huber's liturgical function.

Satisfied, he returned to his position behind the president's head. Looking at the massive wound, Jenkins expressed the futility of their efforts to Perry. "Mac," he said, "we don't have a chance here. Look at this head injury. We cannot resuscitate him." Neurosurgeon Kemp Clark stepped in to examine the gaping hole in the president's skull. A piece of bone, the size of the palm of an adult male, had been blasted out. "There's no possible way. It's too late, Mac," Clark concluded, leaving the neurosurgeon the historical task of declaring the thirty-fifth president dead.[324]

Jackie was standing close by with Dr. George Burkley, the president's personal physician, who had finally gained her access to Jack. She had already wrestled a nurse attempting to get into the room, which had caught Burkley's eye. He went to the fracas in an attempt to persuade Jackie to take some sedation. She would have none of it. "I want to be in there when he dies,"[325] she said. Struck by her sagacity and determination, Burkley led her inside. They stood to the side and watched as the medical team grappled with history. Clark turned to Mrs. Kennedy, "Your husband has sustained a fatal wound," he said.

"I know," came Jackie's near-voiceless reply. Jenkins reached down and drew a sheet over her husband's face.

Burkley, not certain Jackie grasped what Clark had told her, reached over and checked for her husband's pulse. There was none. Holding his face next to hers, he said, "The president is gone." There was no response, and Burkley was now choking back emotion. He wanted to confirm that she understood, and he again leaned into her. "The president is dead." His voice was thick with emotion. Jackie leaned forward, pressing her cheek against his, and Admiral Burkley wept openly.[326]

The room thinned quickly as the bulk of the Parkland staff disappeared. Jenkins remained, removing tubes and IVs and disconnecting the EKG leads. Jackie walked to the end of the table, took her husband's foot in her hand, and kissed it. Moving gently, she moved up his body and softly kissed his leg, then his thigh, before moving to kiss his abdomen, and then his chest. She pulled back the sheet and was now looking upon his face. "His mouth was so beautiful, his eyes were open."[327] She kissed his lips.

Father Huber unscrewed his vial of holy oil and made the sign of the cross on the forehead of the president. He began to pray in Latin, and Jackie took Jack's hand. Softly Jackie responded to the prayers and prayed with the priest the Our Father and Hail Mary prayers of the Catholic rosary. The service complete, Father Huber spoke to Mrs. Kennedy, expressing his "sympathies and the sympathies of his parishioners."

"Thank you," said Jackie in a soft but clear voice. "Thank you for taking care of the president...please pray for him."[328]

"I am convinced that his soul had not left his body," he told her. "This is a valid last sacrament." Bowing her head, she was tilting forward, alarming the priest. "Do you want a doctor?" he asked.[329] An observant nurse brought a cold towel and pressed it against her head, chasing away her dizziness.

Jackie returned to her seat outside the room while Jack's body was prepared for travel. Clint Hill ordered a casket from the O'Neal Funeral Home. "The best damn casket you have," he said, choking out the words. "It's for the president, it's for President Kennedy."[330]

Father Huber and an associate, Father James Thompson, now in the corridor, realized that the gathering press corps awaited them in the parking lot. Across the corridor, Jackie sat. "I will never forget the...agony on her face,"[331] Huber would write, recalling how "she was very much composed... not crying...I couldn't understand how she could hold up under the circumstances."[332]

As Fathers Huber and Thomson crossed the parking lot, a horde of reporters pursued them. Among them was Dallas's KBOX radio news director Bill Hampton, who asked Huber, "Is Mr. Kennedy dead?" Hampton reported, "In his quote, he's dead alright." And just as Huber's quote was hitting the UPI wires, Malcolm Kilduff stood before the press at Parkland Hospital. He had already informed Lyndon Johnson, who had left Parkland bound for Love Field. Kilduff was in Dallas because Press Secretary Pierre Salinger was traveling with cabinet members to the Far East.

Wiping sweat from his brow, the thirty-six-year-old assistant presidential press secretary checked his watch and then firmly pressed his fingertips on the table before him. It was the only way he could stop his hands from shaking. His head bowed, he leaned forward, taking a deep breath. Finding his words, he made the horror official. "President John F. Kennedy died at approximately one o'clock Central Standard time today here in Dallas. He died of a gunshot wound in the brain." The magnanimity of his words swept over him, and his bottom lip began to quiver. Seconds ticked as Kilduff struggled to gather himself. Another deep breath. "I have no other details regarding the assassination of the president."

Lyndon Johnson was safe aboard Air Force I, and he declared he was not leaving Texas without Mrs. Kennedy. Fear, speculation, and chaos ran rampant, with thoughts that an outside force might be attempting to topple the United States government. Every official of the Kennedy administration was now an official of the Johnson administration. Every secretary, every agent, every assistant, and every member of the presidential party held on to their respective titles. Save one.

Just twenty-four hours earlier, Jacqueline Kennedy, the first lady of the United States, had stepped out of Air Force I to a cheering throng at Brooks Air Force Base in San Antonio. She had captivated crowds at every stop in a manner that had been deemed improbable by most and impossible by some. Four hours earlier, she had listened to her husband tell the world that he was "the man who had accompanied Mrs. Kennedy…to Texas."

She now sat alone in a dingy hospital hall, waiting for Jack's body to be placed in a coffin. She no longer formally existed. She was no longer the first lady, and there was no government assignment for the wife of a dead president. The passage of power, which simply shifted every government employee to the administration of Lyndon Johnson, had no provision for a widowed first lady.

"I'm not leaving here without Jack," she whispered to Kenny O'Donnell, while hospital personnel cleaned Jack's corpse. This normally perfunctory routine was anything but perfunctory, for the magnitude of what had transpired began to penetrate all the actors who had played a role in the ghastly, ghoulish play. Each of them was struck by the presence of the shattered leading lady standing lost in their presence. Each wanted to find some way to comfort her, to console her, to soothe her unmitigated anguish.

With the calamity over, the futile fight ended, Jack's men turned to Jackie, seeking to do something. A cup of coffee? A sedative? A place to lie down? All offers she politely and quietly declined. The Parkland personnel reached out as well. A nurse who was washing the body asked if she could get her a towel or help remove her gloves, now stiffening with blood and the remnants of her husband's brains. "No, thank you," came her gentle reply. "I'm all right."

Other actors came to her; powerful men seeking to console and bring comfort literally shattered at her feet. Bill Greer, the driver of the death car, took her face in his hands and, in tears, lamented his role. "Oh Mrs. Kennedy, oh my God, oh my God, I didn't mean to do it, I didn't hear. I should have swerved the car. I couldn't help it...If only I had seen in time." He then put his arms around her and wept on her shoulder. Congressman Henry Gonzalez, a staunch political ally of her husband, came to bring solace, and he, too, crumbled before her. Seeing her fractured core revealed in her eyes, his words vanished, choked off and melted into tears. "Mrs. Kennedy," he stammered, "is there anything I can do for you?" She bowed her head, slowly shaking it no, and it was then he noticed her dress and her gloves covered with the vestiges of her husband. He fell to his knees before her and prayed.

Kenny O'Donnell, awash in his own incalculable anguish, found a mission in the midst of overwhelming despair. For more than a decade, he had served and protected his boss with intense loyalty, which now belonged entirely to the former first lady. Positioning himself in front of her, he shielded her from others' offerings of condolences, and with a ferocity of purpose he diverted them all.

Jackie sat erect, dignified in her frailty. She was feeling faint and in fact had wobbled slightly a number of times. However, those physical manifestations had not diminished her clarity of thought and keen sense of awareness. "Kenny," she said softly to O'Donnell, "get me in there before they close that coffin." And he nodded in affirmation.

Agent Andy Berger signaled to O'Donnell, who bent over and whispered to Jackie, "I want to speak to you," and she followed him. As they attempted to reenter the room, Dr. Kemp Clark appeared. "Please," she said, reaching for the door, "can I go in?" Clark, another powerful man seeking to protect her, shook his head no. Jackie leaned into him. "Doctor," she said, "do you think seeing the coffin can upset me? I've seen my husband die, shot in my arms. His blood is all over me. How can I see something worse than I've seen?" Clark stepped aside.

The room was near empty and smelled of disinfectant. The tumult had dissipated, and so had the assemblage. It was quiet. Kenny O'Donnell stood at the doorway as Dallas police sergeant Robert Dugger walked with Jackie to the president's side. She looked at him, offering her left wrist. The sergeant, vision blurred through tear-filled eyes, finally found the snap of her glove, now stiff with her husband's blood. He slid the glove off her hand. She removed her wedding ring and with Dugger's assistance slipped it on her husband's finger. Satisfied she looked upon him lovingly and returned to Kenny. "Did I do the right thing?" she asked.

"You leave it right where it is," he said.

Vernon O'Neal took command, and with two nurses and an orderly they prepared the president's body for placement in the coffin. Jackie returned to her seat outside in the considerably quieter hall. Jack's friends, agents, and military aides had sealed off the area, affording Jackie as much privacy as the situation would allow. A military aide approached. "You could go back to the plane now," he suggested.

"I'm not going back till I leave with Jack," came her adamant reply. She seated herself and began her vigil, one that would disintegrate into fatuous folly, as another lurid act was still to be staged in the dingy halls of the dreary Dallas hospital.

It began with the arrival of Father Thomas Cain, from the Roman Catholic University of Dallas. No one questioned his presence as he wheeled his car to a stop in the chaos of the parking lot and walked into the hospital. Jackie looked up and there he was. "When did he die?" Father Cain wanted to know.

Startled and careworn, Jackie caught an unsettling look in his eyes. "In the car, I think," she told him.

He reached inside a bag he held in his hand. "I have a relic of the True Cross," he said, and he held it before her. "Venerate it," came his instruction. Somewhat confused, Jackie kissed the cross, and he told her he wanted to take it to the president. "How touching," she thought. "This must mean a lot to him." O'Donnell nodded approval.

The president's body was wrapped and ready to be placed in the coffin when Cain entered and began waving the cross as he walked about the room. Exiting, he said to Jackie, "I have applied a relic of the True Cross to your husband." Jackie noticed he was still holding it. "You didn't even give it to him?" she thought to herself as Kenny O'Donnell, unsettled, moved toward him. The priest reached for Jackie's hand and put his arm around her, calling her Jackie and showering her with terms of endearment. O'Donnell, Dave Powers, and Larry O'Brien were moving toward him as he promised to write her a letter. Noticing the Irish mafia closing in, Cain darted back into the trauma room. He circled O'Neal one more time before exiting to find a group of hospital personnel, whom he led in the Lord's Prayer. Concluding, he returned to Jackie, again reaching for her hand. "Please, Father, leave me alone," she said, pulling away. O'Donnell was now in steady pursuit, and Cain slipped behind a cubicle wall, out of sight, but his voice could be heard frantically reciting prayers.

As Jackie endured the bizarre behavior of the overwrought, unstable cleric, another melodrama was unfolding. Down the hallway and behind closed doors, Dr. Earl Rose, the Dallas County medical examiner, had arrived. He was engaged in what became an intensely heated exchange that began with Agent Roy Kellerman and ultimately included Dr. Burkley, General Godfrey McHugh, Dave Powers, Larry O'Brien, and Ken O'Donnell.

The remains of John F. Kennedy were now in the legal custody of the State of Texas, and Texas statute called for a postmortem. Rose was present to see that it was carried out. Kellerman approached first. "My friend," he said to Rose, "this is the body of the president of the United States, and we are going to take it back to Washington."

Rose would have none of it. "That's not the way things are... There's been a homicide...we must have an autopsy," he emphatically stated, wagging his finger for emphasis.

Taken aback, the agent countered, "He is the president. He's going with us."

"The body stays," came Rose's curt retort, sparking Kellerman's ire.

Maintaining his composure, Kellerman attempted again to reach the dispassionate Rose. "My friend," he began again, "my name is Roy Kellerman. I am special agent in charge of the White House detail of the Secret Service. We are taking President Kennedy back to the capital."

Unmoved, Rose's resolve stiffened. "You're not taking the body anywhere," he fired back. "There's a law here. We're going to enforce it."

Dr. Burkley interjected, appealing to Rose from one physician to another, pleading with him to reconsider. "Mrs. Kennedy is going to stay exactly where she is until the body is moved," he implored. "We can't have that." Rose made it evident that Mrs. Kennedy was free to come and go as she pleased. That was not of his concern. His concern was the corpse of a homicide. "The remains stay."

Burkley's emotions got the best of him, and in his frustration he cried out, "It's the president of the United States!"

This elicited from Rose a pragmatic, "Doesn't matter…can't lose the chain of evidence."

Dave Powers was next, and he simply asked that an exception be made, only to hear, "Regulations." General McHugh stepped in and was told, "There are state laws…you people from Washington can't make your own law."

An appeal was made to the mayor of Dallas, to no avail, leading Burkley to suggest that Rose accompany them back to the nation's capital. This also fell on deaf ears. Outside trauma room one, which still held the body of her husband, now in a coffin, Jackie asked Sergeant Dugger, "Why can't I get my husband back to Washington?" Kellerman had gathered his men, as Dr. Kemp Clark was now exchanging heated, loud words with Rose. Parkland's administrator Charles Price had joined the fray, and Clark was discussing with him the likelihood that Dr. Earl Rose would have to be restrained to allow the body of John F. Kennedy to leave.

Leaving the nurse's station where he was attempting to reach District Attorney Henry Wade, O'Donnell saw Sergeant Dugger positioned near the casket. The Dallas law enforcement officer attempted to call Chief Jesse Curry to implore his intercession in the brewing conflict. Unsuccessful, Dugger was later told that Curry knew it was him and chose not to take his call. The burly sergeant had been "protecting" Jackie since her arrival at Parkland, shooing the horde of Parkland staffers who had gathered to gawk through the window of trauma room one. So moved by the first lady's deportment throughout her ordeal, he understood the anguished, driven desire of Jackie to simply take Jack home, and he wanted to help her. So fierce was his desire that O'Donnell noted his fists were clenched, and he thought to himself, "He's going to belt him." Earl Rose, now in a tantrum, looked ready to hit someone. Powers had secluded Jackie in a cubicle, attempting to shield her from this ultimate indignity. The decision had been made. Kellerman, O'Donnell, and the rest were ready for a physical confrontation, if necessary, to bring their chief home.

A Texas showdown was taking place as the federal contingency, accompanied by Dallas police sergeant Dugger, surrounded the coffin of their chief. Blocking their path, a steadfast Rose, his hand in the air looking like a traffic cop, said again, "You can't leave now! You can't move it!" A Dallas policeman stood beside him, his hand resting on the handle of his holstered pistol.

Approximately forty people now cluttered the hallway as Larry O'Brien and O'Donnell led the casket toward the exit. Dr. Burkley and General McHugh intercepted them. Justice of the Peace Theron Ward was now on the scene, and Burkley and McHugh suggested appealing to him, as he could override the medical examiner. Ward informed them that it was his duty to order an autopsy, which would not take more than three hours. O'Donnell asked if under the circumstances an exception could be made. "It's just another homicide case, as far as I'm concerned," came Ward's reply.

O'Donnell erupted, exploding in a confluence of sadness, frustration, and rage. "Fuck you," he said, now nose to nose with Ward. "We're leaving."

The policeman standing beside Rose intervened. "These two guys [Rose and Ward] say you can't go."

"Get the hell over," came O'Donnell's reply. "We're getting out of here... we're not staying here three hours or three minutes." He called to Powers, "We're leaving now," and turning to Kellerman, he said, "Wheel it out."[333]

A tussle ensued as the coffin was being pushed and pulled in the direction of the exit. Behind Dave Powers, Jackie stepped from her cubicle, her pink suit and nylons stained and matted with the president's blood. She walked behind the coffin. The policeman yielded his place, and Ward returned to the phone in the nurse's station, leaving Earl Rose alone. Jackie emerged, her hand within her white, bloodstained glove resting on Jack's coffin until it reached the ambulance dock to be placed in the waiting hearse.

Clint Hill aided in placing the coffin in the hearse. "We can ride in this car right behind the hearse, Mrs. Kennedy," he said, gently touching her arm.

"No Mr. Hill, I'm riding with the president," came her reply.[334] Sergeant Dugger, who had been by her side throughout her horrendous ordeal, opened the door for her. "Thank you," she whispered to him, and Dugger's eyes filled with tears. It was not the first time they exchanged words. He wanted to offer words of comfort, but they would not come, so he simply offered his hand. Gently, she touched it.

"Bob Dugger, ma'am,"[335] were the only words he could find, and he closed the door. The powerful protector seeking to comfort was comforted. Before the weekend ended, Dugger received a call from the White House expressing gratitude for his kindness.

Clint Hill and Dr. Burkley joined Jackie in the hearse, while Andy Berger took the wheel, telling Vernon O'Neal to follow. It was a high-speed ride back to Air Force I, and along the way Dr. Burkley handed Jackie two red roses. "They were in his shirt," he said. Jackie took them and quietly slipped them into the pocket of her bloodstained suit. In just seven minutes Berger brought the hearse to a halt at the foot of the ramp of the aft section of Air Force I. It was the same ramp from which, just two hours earlier, a glowing Jackie had disembarked while her husband followed, smiling broadly.

The coffin weighed close to half a ton, and all were aware of the daunting task before them. "It's awful heavy," said General Clifton. Looking at the steep steps before them, he added, "Do you suppose we can get it up there?"[336] The question became rhetorical, for without a word spoken, Kenny O'Donnell, Dave Powers, Larry O'Brien, Secret Service agents, and military aides set about to carry their chief aboard his plane. At the foot of the ramp stood a blood-spattered Jackie Kennedy, and behind the entourage stood a lonely Dallas police officer, his cap held over his heart. It took a formidable effort to carry the chief up the steep stairs, only to find his coffin too wide to fit in the door. The men remedied this by breaking the handles to get it on board.

Once on board, Jackie placed a seat as close to Jack as she could before seeking solitude. She wanted just a few minutes alone and made her way down the narrow corridor to the bedroom she and Jack had shared. Opening the door, she froze in mid-step, for laying on the bed was Lyndon Johnson, dictating to his secretary. Johnson sprang up and clumsily brushed past her, quickly followed by Marie Fehmer. Startled, shocked, and confused, she returned to the rear cabin and her seat next to Jack.

Still awash in her husband's blood, Jackie follows Jack's coffin up the stairs of Air Force I. She refused to change her dress wanting "them to see what they've done to Jack." She said later she actually wished she had not washed the blood off her face.

A conflict of leadership existed on the presidential plane. Johnson, unbeknownst to the Kennedy staff, was aboard Air Force I. They thought he was already bound for the capital. Fearful that Dallas authorities would arrive to take custody of President Kennedy's body, they were anxious to get airborne. President Johnson had decided that the plane would not depart until he had been sworn in, and they were waiting for Judge Sarah Hughes to arrive and administer the oath of office. The Kennedy people were shattered. Each having witnessed their boss's murder and/or its grisly aftermath, they now found themselves subjugated by the new president. Adding fuel to the simmering cauldron of sadness and rage was President Johnson's insistence that Jackie be present for his swearing in. O'Donnell thought she was being used, and he resented the request.

Johnson returned to Jackie's vacated bedroom to change his shirt, after which Sergeant Joe Ayres, Air Force I military steward, informed her that he had laid out some towels for her to freshen up. Thanking him she went back to her room, and the Johnsons quickly followed to offer their condolences. Jackie was sitting on the bed, and the president and first lady took a place on either side of her. "Her dress was stained with blood," Lady Bird Johnson recalled. "One leg was almost entirely covered with it and her right glove... was caked with blood—her husband's blood...that immaculate woman, exquisitely dressed and caked in blood." [337] Through her tears, Lady Bird groped for words. "Oh Jackie," she began, "we never even wanted to be vice-president, and now dear God it's come to this."

Jackie, her mind still somewhere in the Dallas motorcade, replied with a question, "Oh what if I hadn't been there?" Through the horror of it all she found solace and answered her own rhetorical question. "I was so glad I was there." She found a scintilla of comfort that the man she loved had died in her arms.

Lady Bird, like everyone who encountered Jackie that day, wanted to do something for her. She recalled, "I asked her if I couldn't get someone in to help her change and she said, 'Oh, no. Perhaps later I'll ask Mary Gallagher but not right now.' And then with almost an element of fierceness—if a person that gentle, that dignified, can be said to have such a quality—she said, 'I want them to see what they have done to Jack.'"[338]

Awkwardness permeated the room. Lyndon Johnson now held the mantle of power and all the responsibilities that came with it. The emotionally ravaged Kennedy people couldn't think beyond the fact that the president, their boss, their friend, was dead, and on some level resented Johnson simply for being alive.

Jackie, however, understood and recognized the difficult role Johnson now had to play, and she put him at ease. "About the swearing in," he cautiously began.

"Lyndon," she said, and quickly caught herself. Realizing the historical aspects of the gut-wrenching events of the day, she continued, "Oh excuse me, I'll never call you that again. I mean, Mr. President."

Downplaying his position, he said, "Honey, I hope you'll call me that [Lyndon] the rest of your life."

An uneasy pause followed, and Johnson brought her back to the moment at hand. "About the swearing in," he repeated.

"Oh yes I know, I know," she replied, "What's going to happen?"

"I've arranged for a judge," explained Johnson. "She'll be here in about an hour. So why don't you lie down…freshen up. We'll leave you alone."

"All right," Jackie said, and they left the room. She lit a cigarette and thought to herself, "My God…an hour?"[339]

Laid out upon her bed was the white suit she was supposed to wear at Friday night's dinner at the governor's mansion. Continually urged to change her clothes, Jackie, with an indomitable will, politely refused every suggestion. The idea of sitting next to her husband's coffin bedecked in white was too vile to even consider. She was steadfastly determined to "let them see what they had done to Jack." Taking the towels off the bed, she entered the powder room, where in a trance-like state she methodically washed Jack's blood from her face and combed his crusted tissue from her hair. The pace of the frenetic madness finally began to dissipate, and with the easing the enormity of it all began to seep in. She did not want to be alone. She wanted to be with those closest to him: Kenny, Dave, Larry, and those who understood the measure of what was lost. She wanted to be with those who could feel her anguish, share her pain, and comprehend the emptiness of her shattered heart.

Judge Hughes arrived, and at the fore of the plane preparations were being made to swear in the thirty-sixth president of the United States. Johnson said they must wait for Mrs. Kennedy, and Pam Turnure thought, "How can they ask her to do this?" Word was sent back to Jackie that all was ready.

"I will be ready in a moment," came her reply, and in Turnure's words, "She just did it."[340]

Jackie stepped out into the corridor, and looking toward the stateroom she saw everybody standing, waiting for her. Confused because only about fifteen minutes had passed since Johnson had told her "about an hour," she paused. Sadness was etched on the faces of the Kennedy staff women, stained with rivers of mascara, and their soft weeping turned to sobs at Jackie's appearance. Johnson went to her, taking her by both hands and leading her down the narrow corridor, backing up as he went. Entering the room, Chief Curry, who less than an hour before had refused Dugger's call, inexplicably offered that the police had done everything they could, an odd comment to a widow whose husband's brains were now crusted on her clothing. Lyndon Johnson placed her at his left arm.

"This is the saddest moment in my life," he said, leaning over her. He quickly introduced her to Judge Hughes, and at Johnson's behest White House photographer Cecil Stoughton placed all the subjects to best photograph the historic moment. "What about a Bible?" came a voice from the assemblage. Joe Ayers remembered that President Kennedy always traveled with a "Catholic missile" and headed to the bedroom, retrieving it from the drawer at his bedside table.

From Sarah Hughes' utterance, "I do solemnly swear," to Lyndon Johnson's, "So help me God," took only twenty-eight seconds. Twenty-eight interminable seconds, after which the president embraced his wife and then kissed the widow's cheek. Lady Bird, fighting tears, took Jackie's hand and guided her to the seat upon which Stoughton stood to capture history. "Sit here, Honey," she said to Jackie.[341] In a firm voice, indicating his first official presidential order, Johnson said simply, "Now let's get airborne."[342] With that, Colonel James Swindal rolled his plane toward the runway and at 2:47 p.m., two hours and seventeen minutes after shots rained down on Dealey Plaza, Air

Jackie stands at the side of Lyndon Johnson as he is sworn in as Jack's successor. In shock and devastated, she remained mindful of the importance of the continuity of government. Many in the Kennedy inner circle were irate at Johnson for asking her to stand with him.

Force I lifted off, taking John F. Kennedy home. White House pool reporter Sid Davis, one of three reporters who stood witness to history, remembered, "She was unblinking, in grief...she knew exactly what was going on, she felt it was important...and she had to be in that room." Reflecting, he offered, "In the annals of history it was one of the most courageous things I've ever seen."[343]

Jackie excused herself and returned to Jack's side. Kenny, Dave, Larry, and General McHugh were standing around the coffin. Kenny, who had remained next to his boss during the swearing in of his successor, took a vacant seat next to Jackie. Their eyes met, unleashing a deluge of tears. Jackie's sobs were heard above the roar of the engines as, for ten minutes or more, her soul released its anguish. Kenny didn't move as these two wounded vessels sat side by side, each consumed with their shared and separate agony. Finally, Jackie regained her voice.

As the adrenaline dissipated, the burden of what had transpired descended on her, and as if awakening she uttered softly, "Oh, it's happened."

"It's happened," came O'Donnell's benumbed reply.

"Kenny...what's going to happen?" she inquired.

O'Donnell, lost in his own cauldron of sadness and rage, shot back, "Jackie...I don't give a damn."

Jackie sighed, "You're right...you're right. Nothing matters but what you've lost."[344]

The transcendent horror of Dealey Plaza swallowed what had been a transformative experience for Jack and Jackie Kennedy. The carnage of the presidential limousine obliterated the warmth of the joyous outpouring of the citizens of Texas. The wave of affection that had begun in San Antonio, carried into Houston, reached a frenzy in Fort Worth, and culminated in Dallas had exceeded any and every expectation. And in just six seconds, adulation turned to abomination, ravaging the joyful hope that filled Jackie's heart—the hope that springs from a deeper understanding of one's self and the world in which we live; the hope born of a love that had reached a new depth in knowing that she and her husband were about to turn the page on mistakes and tragedies of the past; the hope born of a future that, on this Friday morning, glimmered with a sparkle and brilliance she had not known before; and the hope of more children that had filled her heart at the dawn of this day. All of that was gone, forever.

Air Force I carried two presidents back to the nation's capital. The thirty-sixth president occupied the state room, where most of the talk focused on the continuity of government. In the aft of the plane, Jackie Kennedy sat next to the coffin. The Irish mafia did not leave her side. Space was limited, and there was but one chair next to Jackie. O'Brien and Powers stood throughout the flight, while O'Donnell intermittently sat next to her.

Jackie Kennedy now occupied a singularly unique place in American history, having stood at the arm of two presidents as they swore to "preserve, protect and defend" the United States Constitution. Now as she sat next to Jack's coffin, sharing reminiscences with his dearest friends, she began to formulate the pageantry of his funeral, taking her first step to preserve, protect, and defend his legacy.

As Colonel Swindal, battling tears, piloted Air Force I home to a shocked and grieving capital, Jackie set about to do just that. Malcolm Kilduff, whom President Kennedy had playfully nicknamed "McDuff," was summoned. "Mac," she instructed him, "you make sure...you go and tell them that I came back here and sat with Jack."[345] Kilduff assured her he would do so. Throughout the flight, various Kennedy staffers made their way back to pay their respects to Jackie as the two-hour and eighteen-minute ride home took on the characteristics of an Irish wake.

She remembered how much Jack loved the voice of Boston tenor Luigi Vena. Vena sang at their wedding in Newport ten Septembers earlier, and recalling that day Jackie decided he would sing at Jack's funeral. The "Ave Maria," which Jack and Jackie listened to kneeling together in the sanctuary of St. Mary's, would waft over his coffin and the congregation of St. Matthew's Cathedral in Washington, D.C. Of course Cardinal Cushing would preside, and it would be a low Catholic mass to lessen the pomposity. Jack preferred that to the solemnity of the high ritual.

Dave's mind wandered back just one month to Jack's last trip to Boston and his last visit with his dad. Jackie sat with rapt attention as Dave described their parting. Since impaired by a stroke suffered in December 1961, the ambassador's wheelchair was wheeled onto his porch to watch the chopper land and to say goodbye to his son when it departed. An early morning fog had dissipated, and Jack made his way across the lawn. He "went to his father, put his arms around the old man's shoulders and kissed his forehead." He started to walk away, then paused and "went back and kissed him a second time" before coming aboard. Jack was looking at his dad through the window of Marine I, a man once among the world's most powerful men but now frail and debilitated. Dave saw tears come to Jack's eyes, and he said, "He's the one who made all this possible and look at him now."

"It almost seemed," Dave said to Jackie, "as if the president knew he was seeing his father for the last time." [346]

Kenny could not shake from his mind the conversation he, Jack, and Jackie had had just six hours earlier in suite 850 in Fort Worth's Hotel Texas. "You know what, Jackie?" O'Donnell said. "Can you tell me why we were saying that this morning? What was it...Last night would have been a great night to assassinate a president? Can you tell me why we were talking about that? I've never discussed that with him in my life." [347] Jackie just shook her head; none of it mattered anyway.

Evelyn Lincoln, Jack's longtime secretary, came back to offer comfort, but as everyone else that day, she could not find the words, stammering out a banal, "Everything's going to be all right."

"Oh, Mrs. Lincoln," replied Jackie as Kenny sprang from his chair. One thing both Kenny and Jackie knew was "all right" would never be the same.

"You know what I'm going to have, Jackie?" Kenny said. "I'm going to have a helluva stiff drink." He suggested she join him.

Jackie was hesitant, fearful that alcohol would unleash the torrent of emotion that consumed her. "What will I have?" she asked.

"I'll make you a scotch," he said.

"I've never had scotch in my life," came her tentative reply before giving Kenny an affirmative nod. Turning to General McHugh, she said, "Now is as good a time as any to start."

Kenny brought her a tall glass, which, despite its acerbity, she finished and then drank another.[348] In the true tradition of an Irish wake, the liquor flowed and flowed freely; however, none of it seemed to have any effect. The deepest feelings of grief and loss simply could not be assuaged.

The reminiscence continued as Powers recalled their trip to Ireland the previous June and how Jack had loved the Irish songs sung together. As Dave recalled "Danny Boy" and "Kelly, the Boy from Killane," Jackie said wistfully, "He said it was the most enjoyable experience of his whole life," and she wished she'd been there. Jackie recalled how impressed Jack was by the Irish cadets. "I must have those Irish cadets at his funeral," she said, and her mind drifted to just last week when she had invited Scotland's Black Watch to perform on the White House lawn. "He loved the Black Watch pipers," she said. "They must be there, too." The Black Watch of the Royal Highlanders Regiment followed Jackie in her march behind Jack's caisson, and the Irish cadets greeted the caisson upon its arrival at Arlington.[349]

Twenty-five years later, Powers recalled that wretched flight back from Dallas on that wretched day. At one point in the conversation, Jackie looked at Powers. "What will you do now, Dave? You were with him for all these years."

"I was so proud of her," said Powers. "She was holding us together. I never felt so bad about anything in my life." The pain of his loss was clearly visible on his face and audible in his voice. It was a loss that a quarter of a century had not mitigated.[350] She touched each member of Jack's famous

Irish mafia. "You were with him at the start and you're with him at the end," she told them.

Larry O'Brien recalled, "That frail girl...bringing to the surface some strength within her while we three slobs dissolved."[351]

This was the second time she had done this. Just before she joined Lyndon and Lady Bird Johnson for his swearing in, she had summoned Agent Clint Hill, her primary protector, who just two hours earlier had leaped on the back of the limousine, in all probability saving her life. Making his way to her, Hill was overcome with a sense of guilt and shame. "How could I let this happen to her?" he was thinking as he approached her[352]. "Yes, Mrs. Kennedy, what do you need?"

She took his hands in hers, looked into his eyes, and asked, "What's going to happen to you now, Mr. Hill?"

Tears filled his eyes, and gaining control of his trembling lip he uttered, "I'll be okay, Mrs. Kennedy, I'll be okay." "With all the sorrow and heartbreak," Hill thought to himself, "to have concern for me at this time, she really is a remarkable lady."[353]

Dave and Kenny again spoke of Jack's last trip to Boston. They had gone to Harvard Stadium to watch his alum take on Columbia. The first half came to an end, and Jack grabbed Dave. "I want to go to Patrick's grave," he told him, "and I want to go alone with nobody from the newspapers following me."[354] They rose to leave, and with the press in hot pursuit, Kenny went to the cop in charge of the parking lot. The officer saw to it that no press cars left the lot until the president's car was far out of sight. Arriving at the new Kennedy family plot in Brookline, they made their way to the grave, where they stood silently. "He seems so alone here," Jack said.[355]

"I'll bring them together now," Jackie said slowly, nodding her head.[356]

Overtures continued in an attempt to get Jackie to change her bloodstained suit. In the state room it was a topic of concern and conversation between agent Rufus Youngblood and President Johnson. General McHugh approached her and simply asked, "Why not change?" Jackie gave her head a forceful shake. Mary Gallagher approached Kenny, offering to help Jackie "clean up."

"If she wants to stay this way for five days," said Kenny, "it'll show the world what's been done to Jack."[357]

Dr. Burkley noticed that Jackie's gold bracelet still wore remnants of the carnage of the limousine, and one more time he tried. Kneeling in front of her, he held out his trembling hand. "Another dress?" he modestly suggested. Jackie responded in a whisper that was emphatic, firm, decisive, and clear. "No, let them see what they've done to Jack!" The ferocity Lady Bird had seen in her grew in its intensity with each suggestion that she change.

That matter clearly settled, Kilduff tried another approach, suggesting to Jackie that they deplane on the opposite side. The coffin and those surrounding it would be blocked from view by the plane itself. Most important to Kilduff was keeping photographers from capturing Jackie, smeared with her husband's blood. She politely listened and then said, "We'll go out the regular way…I want them to see what they've done."[358] The course of action firmly established, Kilduff and Jackie's conversation continued as, through tears, he told her of the recent death of his four-year-old son, Kevin, who had drowned while Kilduff was traveling with the president in Europe. Another man of power was comforted in her company.

The chaos of Dallas continued aboard Air Force I. Through garbled, oft-repeated, and unintelligible radio transmissions, generals, admirals, and captains arranged the logistics for the continuity of government and President Kennedy's autopsy. While some were arranging a helicopter to Bethesda Naval Hospital, others were calling for a hearse to Walter Reed Army Hospital. Seated next to her husband's coffin, Jackie had already decided "Bethesda," in a Navy ambulance. Jack was after all a Navy man.

The conversation moved, for the first time, to the place of burial. Virtually everyone assumed it would be in Boston. It was, after all, home, and Jackie had mentioned she would bring her son and husband together now. She heard their voices, but she was lost in the memory of a conversation she'd had with him two years prior, after she returned to the White House following the funeral of a friend. "He must be buried in Boston," said Kenny, "and don't you let them change it."

Absorbed in her own agony and dazed in grief, she nodded, remembering their conversation. "Where will we be buried…Jack?" she had asked him.

"Hyannis, I guess," he replied. "We'll all be there."

"I think you should be buried in Arlington," she said. "You…belong to all of the country."

Jack made a characteristic self-deprecating comment about pharaohs' tombs. He did belong to all the country, which, forty thousand feet below him, was now focused on their murdered president, his widow, and when they would land in Washington.[359]

The day's darkness gave way to night as Air Force I approached Andrews Air Force Base. Still scrambling through the logistics of deplaning, uncertainty reigned. Who would walk down which ramp? What was protocol? President Johnson would speak, as exhibiting government continuity was a paramount concern. This was why Jackie, through the numbness of her personal agony, chose to stand with Johnson when he took the oath. The world would witness the unwavering United States government in the hands of the new president. However, it was equally clear that the deportment of Jacqueline Kennedy would leave its own indelible mark. The presidency belonged to Lyndon Johnson, but it was the thirty-four-year-old widow who held the hearts of his people.

Chaos and confusion now spilled over to those on the ground at Andrews. An honor guard had gathered to receive the body of their commander-in-chief. TV reporters were telling their viewers that the body would be flown by helicopter to Bethesda Naval Hospital.

Approaching Andrews, Dave Powers sought out Agent Roy Kellerman. His eyes filled with tears. "Roy," he began, "Mrs. Kennedy wanted me to tell you she would like the agents who worked for President Kennedy, along with those of us on his staff, to carry the casket off the aircraft." Struggling to maintain his composure, he continued, "And she wants Bill Greer to drive the vehicle...to transport the president to Bethesda Naval Hospital. She said how much Jack loved...all of you and she knows how much you're suffering."[360]

Colonel Swindal brought Air Force I to rest, and the ramp was wheeled into place at the front of the plane. As staff members disembarked, a shadowy figure battled his way up the stairs to get on the plane. Attorney General Robert Kennedy had but one thing on his mind: get to Jackie. Tears streaming down his face, passing by people he never really saw, he worked his way to the rear of the plane and found her. "Jackie," he said, placing his arm around her. "I'm here."[361] They embraced and wept in each other's arms. The door swung open, and a yellow truck, equipped with a hydraulic lift, nestled under the rear door, the same door Jack and Jackie had exited merely hours before.

"There's a helicopter here to take you to the White House," Bobby informed her. "Don't you want to do that?"

"No, no," she softly replied. "I just want to go to Bethesda." And catching a glimpse of the gray ambulance, she said, "We'll just go in that."[362]

A six-member honor guard, representing each group of the U.S. military, waited to bear the body of their fallen leader. Powers, O'Brien, and O'Donnell led the contingent as they struggled to move their boss. As gently as the coffin's weight allowed, they rested it in the hydraulic box and waited to be lowered. The lowering complete, Powers and O'Brien lifted each corner to the edge of the lift. As Powers jumped, fifteen men scurried towards them, reaching for the coffin. Among them was the honor guard, without ceremony and absent of formation; some assisted in the coffin's removal and then deferred to the men in suits, who eased the coffin into the back of the U.S. Navy ambulance. Jackie appeared, hand in hand with

Bobby, covered with the dark stains of Jack's blood. The world witnessed "what they had done to Jack."

Angier Biddle Duke, the White House chief of protocol, recalled the scene twenty-five years later. "It was a stark scene...devoid of ceremony... almost ugly in its reality...no speeches, no words. It was purely functional, mechanical...To see the coffin go into a vehicle...Mrs. Kennedy put in a car. Not a word was said by anybody...It was one of the lowest points...in anybody's lives."[363]

With assistance from Bobby and Clint Hill, Jackie half jumped and was half lifted to the ground. She gracefully walked to the ambulance, grasping the rear door handle, which was locked. Several men sprang into action opening the door, allowing her and Bobby to enter the back. A helicopter was waiting to take her to the White House, but Jackie was still not ready to leave Jack.

As requested, Bill Greer got behind the wheel of the ambulance as those whom "Jack loved and who were suffering" slid their chief to rest in the back of the ambulance. Although teeming with mind-numbing grief, Jackie orchestrated Jack's final egress. The ugly, misshapen exit, though awash in chaos, was engulfed in symbolism, choreographed by Jackie. The gray Navy ambulance rolled away from: the lights, the cameras, the assembled congressional delegation, and the first public statement of the nation's thirty-sixth president. "This is a sad time for all people," Lyndon Johnson droned into the microphones. "We have suffered a loss that cannot be weighed. For me it is a deep personal tragedy. I know the world shares the sorrow that Mrs. Kennedy and her family bear. I will do my best that is all I can do. I ask for your help, and God's."

They sat inches from Jack. Jackie, haunted with the day's mental images and Bobby choked with anguish, both racked with grief. Transfixed and looking past her brother-in-law, Jackie recounted the horrors of Dealey Plaza and

Parkland Hospital. Bobby, keenly aware of her need to purge, sat quietly listening as, for twenty minutes, she vividly spilled the gruesome details of her odious ordeal. The ride through Washington for him was a trip through the fifteen-year journey he had shared with his brother from the halls of Congress to the White House.

They arrived at Bethesda's front entrance, and for the first time since she entered the rear of the limousine at Love Field, Jackie left Jack. He was bound for the morgue and she to a suite on the seventeenth floor, where family and intimates were gathering. Already waiting were Jean Kennedy Smith, Ben and Toni Bradlee, Jackie's mom and Hughdie, and Nancy Tuckerman. Jean was looking out the window when someone said, "She's here." Ben Bradlee turned, and "there was a totally doomed child, with that God-awful skirt, not saying anything, looking burned alive." Jackie fell sobbing into his arms. Toni and her mom came forward, each offering a word or a touch. Jackie embraced Nancy Tuckerman, relaying how sad it was that she had left her home in New York "to take this job...and now it's all over." "Tucky," as Jackie called her, was awestruck that in the midst of it all Jackie was thinking of her.

Once again she endured the onslaught of suggestions that she change and/or take a sedative, and once again she remained steadfast in her desire to do neither. All she wanted to do was talk. Dr. John Walsh urged that they "leave her alone" and "let her talk herself out." Talk she did, and once again the nightmare unfolded. She told Walsh of the limousine, Toni and Ben Bradlee of her wedding ring, and then she spoke of Patrick's death. Listening from a distance, Ethel Kennedy whispered to Ben, "How does she do it?" to which Bradlee replied, "She's purging herself."

"It's the best way," suggested Dr. John Walsh. "Let her get rid of it, if she can."

Defense Secretary Robert McNamara arrived after meeting with President Johnson, and he became yet another vessel for Jackie to fill with the minutia of her nightmare in Dallas. "She was in that suit," McNamara recalled, "with the bloody skirt and blood all over her stockings...she just wanted someone to talk to...We were in the kitchen, Jackie sitting on a stool and me on the floor...I was concentrating entirely upon her because she needed me." Leaving Jackie, the secretary joined the conversation regarding Jack's burial. Powers, O'Donnell, and O'Brien were now steadfast in their desire for a Massachusetts burial, and Jean concurred. Bradlee, a native Bostonian, was not on board, nor was McNamara, who said so to Bobby. At Bobby's urging he returned to Jackie in the kitchen and offered her his thoughts on the president's final resting place. "A president, particularly this president, who has done so much for the nation's spiritual growth and enlarged our horizons and who was martyred this way, belongs in a national environment." [364] This was and had always been Jackie's inclination, and although she was leaning that way, her mind was on the more immediate tasks at hand: getting Jack home to the White House and the services for Saturday.

William Walton was at the White House assisting Sargent Shriver with funeral plans. He received a message from Jackie: "Just make it as much like Lincoln's as possible." Walton called the Library of Congress, requesting "all visual material that's possible." They delivered the material right away, and Walton then called several local department stores, procuring "hundreds of yards of black material." The coup de grace for Walton came "when we found Lincoln's catafalque...that his coffin had rested on...and put it up." [365]

At about 10:00 p.m., Charlie and Martha Bartlett, who had introduced Jack and Jackie, arrived, and Jackie repeated the terrible tale of the motorcade to Charlie. "I gathered she had been talking about it a long time," he said, and he was taken by the depth of her poise, as her "tears were just a breath away, but they never came." [366]

Kenny O'Donnell could not get the ring off his mind. Throughout the flight it gnawed at him, and he couldn't shake the thought that she should have it. On the day in which the glowing light of hope had been stolen by repugnant wickedness, he wanted to restore some tenderness. He approached Jackie. "I'm going to get that ring back for you," he told her, and he left the suite, descending to the morgue below where he found Dr. Burkley and expressed his wish. Following the autopsy and before Jack was embalmed, Burkley removed the ring. Upstairs, he requested of Bobby that he be allowed to return it to her personally, and with Bobby's blessing, he entered the small bedroom. He handed Jackie the ring. She expressed her gratitude and that of her husband for all he had done for the president, and then reaching into the pocket of her skirt, she removed a rose he had given her when they were riding in the hearse from the hospital to Love Field. Taken, once again, by the depth and measure of her thoughtfulness and compassion, he struggled to speak. Through his tear-filled heart, he said, "This is the greatest treasure of my life."[367]

The arrival of the body back at the White House was initially projected to be at about 11:00 p.m. However, eleven o'clock melted into midnight and far beyond. And as the night crept toward dawn, two camps worked on the majesty to follow. At Bethesda there was Jackie, Bobby, and Secretary McNamara, while at the White House it was Shriver, Walton, and Richard Goodwin.

Many were huddled in the bedroom. The TV, tuned to NBC, droned as Robert MacNeil reported that a suspect was charged in the president's murder. It was approaching midnight when he handed off to Frank McGee, who chronicled the tragedies of the Kennedy family, culminating with Jackie's three lost pregnancies and "today the loss of her husband...The thoughts and sympathies of all of us are with the first lady." He then concluded his broadcast, "There is no way of calculating the millions of words that have been uttered during the course of this day...I seriously doubt that any words uttered by anyone, anywhere have succeeded in expressing what you feel yourself." He paused, clearing his throat as he struggled to choke out his words, "The answer for that is only to be found in the hearts of each of us."[368]

The room grew silent, and the gathering began to dissipate. Jackie, sitting around the kitchen table that intermittently included Toni, Martha, Jean, Ethel, Marge McNamara, Pam Turnure, and Nancy Tuckerman, had finally "talked out" the details of the assassination, and the conversation had moved on to the details of the funeral. "I am going to walk behind the casket," she told Turnure. "Whatever procession there was, the one thing she wanted to do was to walk behind it, and considering the emotional state she was in…she was thinking of all sorts of details and other people…instead of waiting to be told…she was already thinking about how it must be done."

"She was very much in command of herself," recalled Tuckerman. "Obviously…in a certain amount of shock, but she could operate and she could make sense, and she realized that she had to make certain decisions and she did them simply beautifully."[369]

She was now doing her best to simply be a gracious hostess, once again refusing a sedative and her mother's suggestion to change. "It was," thought Martha Bartlett, "as if she didn't want the day to end."[370]

Friday, November 22, was drawing to a close, and Ben and Toni Bradlee were the first to leave the Bethesda suite. Jackie, ever gracious, suggested that Pam, Nancy, Evelyn Lincoln, and Mary Gallagher go home and get some sleep. "Somehow," she said, "we've got to get through the next few days. Be strong for two or three days, then we'll all collapse."[371]

There was no sleep for Pam or Nancy as they returned to the White House to assist Walton and his work crew. "William Walton was there with books he had gotten from the Library of Congress, showing how the room had looked at the time of Lincoln's funeral, and we spent a great deal of time putting up this black crepe paper around the mantel piece, and…the chandeliers…until about three in the morning."[372]

Forever steadfast and determined, Jackie made it clear that she would not be "leaving here until Jack goes," and Dr. Walsh was growing increasingly concerned for her. Thirty-six hours ago she had awakened early in the White

House, beginning a frenetic day that took her through three Texas cities before ending after 1:00 a.m. in Fort Worth. She was now approaching a twenty-hour day that began in Fort Worth and deteriorated into the rigors of a nightmare that seemed to have no end. Long, emotionally grueling days awaited her, and he was worried just how long she could endure. She had talked herself out and refused Bobby's suggestion that she return to the White House. Walsh approached her with a needle containing one hundred milligrams of the sedative Visatril. He showed it to her.

"Just give me something so I could have a little nap," she said, holding out her arm. Convinced this would take hold in less than a minute, he administered the shot, found a chair, and instantaneously was asleep.[373] Ten minutes later he was startled by Jackie walking past his chair looking for a pack of cigarettes. She smiled at the look of astonishment on his face, and Walsh knew his patient would not sleep this night.

No less than twenty-five people had joined the crew of Shriver, Walton, and Goodwin preparing the East Room to welcome home their chief. It was the artist Walton to whom all had deferred, and he directed the laying of black crepe as it lay neigh a century ago around the body of Abraham Lincoln. At Bethesda, Jackie, Bobby, and McNamara were discussing funeral details. Jackie "wanted the coffin closed."

"It can't be done," they countered. "Everybody wants to see a Head of State."

"I don't care," she replied. "It's the most awful morbid thing, they have to remember Jack alive."[374] Jackie fell silent, which was mistaken for consent.

It was 4:34 a.m. when the Marine Deathwatch greeted their president as Bill Greer drove the chief through the front gates of the White House for the final time. Exiting the car Jackie and Bobby were greeted by their brother-in-law, Sargent Shriver, who took their hands as the honor guard got into place to carry the president home. They followed the coffin through the front door and down the hallway toward the East Room, where the catafalque came into view. She entered the room behind the coffin and stood watching as, beneath the portraits of George and Martha Washington, Jack was placed upon the bier. The honor guard in place, an altar boy lit four candles, and then Father John Kuhn of St. Matthews' offered a prayer. "Out of the depths I cry to you, O Lord; Lord hear my voice," he intoned. Jackie stood stoic, still wearing her husband's blood on the pink suit she'd donned nearly twenty-

It was 4:30 a.m. when Jackie, still in her blood-stained pink suit, brought Jack home to lie in state in the East Room, bedecked in black precisely as it had been when Lincoln lay there a century earlier. Hugh and Janet Auchincloss stand third and fourth from left.

four hours earlier. The prayer finished, and she knelt at the head of the coffin, reached under the flag, lifted it, and buried her face in its field of stars.

Her deplorable, despicable, daunting day was over. Jack was home. She stood, walked back through the hallway and up the stairs, leaving Bobby to view the body and learn what she already knew: the coffin would be closed.

Dawn's first light was leaking through the gray clouds when she reached her private quarters. Provi Paredes, her longtime aide, was waiting for her, and they exchanged a tear-filled embrace. Finally, with Provi's help, she removed her suit and sank into a bath. Sleep was still illusive. Dr. Walsh prepared another injection, which he administered to her after her bath. She lay upon her bed and wept until finally she drifted off to sleep. It was just short of twenty-four hours since she had awakened in suite 850 of the Hotel Texas in Fort Worth.

Light came to the morning of November 23, but there was no sun, only murky gray skies that, as if in a release of cosmic anguish, poured down a steady, soaking rain throughout most of the day. Jackie's sleep was but a nap; at 8:15 a.m. she was speaking to Caroline and John, trying to make sense of the insensible. Caroline knew her daddy was gone. Maud Shaw had told her. Just after 7:00 a.m., she entered her daddy's room and found granmère Janet and Uncle Hughdie. "She had her big giraffe with her," Janet remembered, "and John came in pulling some toy." Pointing to a picture of her father covering the newspaper's front page, Caroline asked, "Who is that?"

"Oh, Caroline," said Janet. "You know that's your daddy."

"He's dead, isn't he?" came her rhetorical inquiry. "A man shot him, didn't he?"[375]

Janet could only nod. "A bad man shot daddy," Jackie told her son and then caught herself, clarifying that he really wasn't bad, merely "sick."[376] When told that daddy had gone to heaven, John simply wanted to know when he was coming back.

The East Room ceremonies began with a private mass for the family at 10:00 a.m., marking the first collective gathering of family and close friends. Throughout the service, quiet crying gave way to sobs and an occasional wail. The book of Isaiah tells us "a child shall lead them," and in the East Room of the White House on a dreary rainy November Saturday, a six-year-old little girl sought to lead her mother through her anguish. As the mass was coming to an end, Uncle Sarge was behind Caroline and Jackie, who were kneeling together. Following prayer Jackie stood, and Shriver observed a "mask of agony." Standing with her, "Caroline took Jackie's left hand in her right hand...patted her mother's hand and looked up with an expression of intelligence and compassion and love, trying to comfort her mother."

An impromptu receiving line formed, waiting to express condolences to the widow as they passed out of the room and into the hall. Dutifully, Jackie stood, offering words of gratitude and affection for the fierce loyalty each had given her husband. Some couldn't bear to hear them. Ben Bradlee left the room, and Red Fay simply stood back, lingering, watching the rain fall outside the window. Just as she had on Air Force I's flight the day before, she was, in Powers' words, "holding us together."

This effort drained her both physically and emotionally; however, her compassion was unyielding when the White House chief usher Bernard West approached her. He was the last in the line. He stood speechless, trying to capture words that simply eluded him. In her own anguish she managed a faint smile. "Poor Mr. West," she said. "Will you walk with me...over to his office?" Words stuck in his throat. West could only nod, and the two of them, along with Clint Hill, made the silent, short walk to the Oval Office.

Jackie had overseen a remodeling, the particulars of which she had kept from Jack so he would be surprised when he returned from Texas. She wanted to check on some of Jack's personal items. The room was already being packed, and Jackie felt in the way. West took notes of the items Jackie wanted; among them were the encased coconut shell from Jack's PT 109 rescue, his scrimshaw collection, and family photos. As she left, Jackie walked by his rocking chair and softly ran her hand over it.

Throughout the remainder of Saturday, a collection of mourners paid their respects. The Kennedy appointees, the cabinet, and the White House staff were followed by the Supreme Court, then the Senate, House, governors and, finally, Washington's chiefs of diplomatic missions.

Jackie returned to the second-floor living quarters, where she would remain throughout most of the day, choreographing her husband's funeral. A firestorm of protest came when she chose St. Matthew's Cathedral over the Shrine of the Immaculate Conception. The assumption of all was that the Shrine, the largest cathedral in North America, would be the obvious choice. It was majestic, regal, and held 2,500 people. Knowing that the hierarchy of the church would be disappointed did not dissuade her. She was unimpressed with the Shrine and knew that, despite the fact that it was antiquated and by comparison raggedy, St. Matthew's was the right choice because it held memories of masses they had attended there together. She also intended to walk behind the caisson to the church.

This brought a cacophony of discord. Angie Duke and the Secret Service were added to the list of those telling her why walking couldn't and/or shouldn't be done. Her intention was to walk from the White House to St. Matthew's and then from the church to Arlington. It was just under a mile to the church, but Arlington was a little over three miles. Duke was not sure this would fall in line at all with American protocol. He wasn't sure there was a precedent for it. Added to that were the heads of state who would fall in behind her, and Duke was facing a protocol nightmare the likes of which had never been seen. As for the Secret Service, still stuck in the throes of what had transpired a scant twenty-four hours earlier, they were beyond leery of President Johnson and a host of government officials, including Jackie, being exposed in such a manner.

Duke was satisfied about the Americanism of the walk when he learned that processions had walked behind the coffins of Washington, Lincoln,

Grant, and Teddy Roosevelt. His attentions now turned to the protocol for the walking heads of state. The joint chiefs of staff were Jackie's only ally in this effort, for in the minds of warriors there could be no more fitting tribute than to march behind the caisson of their fallen commander.

It was General Clifton who appealed to her to reconsider. "Gentlemen," he told her, "would not remain seated while the widowed first lady was on foot...and few of these gentlemen were fit for such a hike." In his pragmatic plea he reminded her that behind her would be members of Congress, many of them septuagenarians and octogenarians, not to mention many aging heads of state as well. Thoughtfully considering Clifton's plea, she offered a compromise. Abandoning the walk from St. Matthew's to Arlington, she would only walk to St. Matthew's. Others still pushed to forsake the entire idea of walking, but as she had been since Dallas, she remained resolute. Those unable to walk could be driven to St. Matthew's beforehand, and she offered, "Nobody has to walk but me."

Still pushing, someone asked, "What if it rains?"

"I don't care," came her reply. "I'll walk anyway."[377] Her unwavering, insistent tone put the matter to rest.

However, the Secret Service was, to say the least, anxious. Gerald Behn, the agent in charge of the White House detail, summoned Clint Hill. "Clint...you must explain to her how dangerous this will be...It's a security nightmare. You've got to convince her this is a bad idea...We'll be sitting ducks.[378] This funeral is going to stretch our security capabilities to the max as it is. Will you please try to talk her out of it? You're the only one who even has a chance."[379]

Hill knew her better than any member of the Secret Service, and though he thought the idea of her walking "insane," he also understood and respected her need to do it. He knew that his plea would fall on deaf ears; however, he did his duty. After calling Jackie, he made his way upstairs, where she was waiting for him.

"Hello Mr. Hill, come in," she said with profound sadness etched in her face. They exchanged cordialities, and Hill got to the point of his visit.

"Mrs. Kennedy," he began, "I've been told you intend to walk in the funeral possession...and I wanted to clarify what exactly it is that you intend to do."

"Oh Mr. Hill," she replied. "Don't worry, I've decided not to walk all the way, only from the White House to St. Matthew's."

Not quite satisfied with half a loaf, Hill pressed. "Mrs. Kennedy, there's a lot of concern about other people who might decide to walk, if you walk."

"Well, Mr. Hill," she said, "they can ride or do whatever they want to. I'm walking behind the president to St. Matthew's."

The firmness of purpose he heard in her voice affirmed what he already knew, and he thanked her for seeing him and returned to his office. "Gerry," he said to Behn, "she does intend to walk...but only from the White House to St. Matthew's."

Behn beseeched Hill again. "No chance to talk her out of it, Clint?"

Hill laid the matter to rest once and for all. "Believe me, Gerry, nothing is going to change her mind. She is walking."[380]

Through the incessant rain, friends, dignitaries, and White House staff arrived in the East Room, where the flag-draped coffin lay beneath the chandelier shrouded in black crepe. Black crepe also framed the mantle and the windows. Outside the people stood—hundreds, maybe thousands—beyond the White House gates. Some were under umbrellas, some not, watching, each paying his or her own silent tribute to the slain president.

As Saturday morning creeped toward afternoon, virtually all believed that President Kennedy would be buried at home in Massachusetts. Protocol officer Angie Duke, in referencing the death of FDR and his subsequent burial at his home in Hyde Park, New York, asked, "What's the Hyde Park of the Kennedy family?"[381] The answer, of course, was Brookline, where baby Patrick lay at rest. All that appeared to still be decided was if the president would make his final journey by train, by plane, or by sea.

Three people, however, still had Arlington on their minds: Robert McNamara, Arlington superintendent John Metzler, and the president's widow. Responding to two different radio reports suggesting Arlington as a possibility, Metzler visited early on Saturday, selecting three possible gravesites. McNamara was in his office at 6:00 a.m., and before the East Room mass, he had already met Metzler and been shown the three designations. As the mass came to an end, McNamara found Bobby, his sisters Jean and Pat, and Bill Walton, informing them of his morning foray and suggesting they come with him on a return visit. Walton and McNamara took a cab, and the Kennedys followed in a White House car. The morning mist had become a chilling steady rain, and when the tour ended, the consensus was that the Arlington hillside overlooking the Potomac and the nation's capital would be the perfect place for Jack to rest. As if by some mystical, cosmic guidance, Walton's artistic eye noted that the chosen spot lay precisely on the invisible axis between the Custis Lee mansion atop the hill and the Lincoln Memorial across the river.

Upon their return, Jean told Jackie, "We've found the most wonderful place," and Jackie knew the time had come. Jackie and Bobby joined Jean and Pat while Walton, Billings, and Jim Reed followed. Stopping at the Pentagon to pick up McNamara, it was on to Arlington, where Metzler waited in a freezing, pelting rain. "We went out and walked to that hill," Jackie told William Manchester, "and of course you knew that's where it should be." Jackie glanced at Walton and gave him a nod, after which Walton and Metzler slogged their way up the soggy hillside.

Walton stood for a moment eyeing the mansion at the top of the hill and the memorial to Lincoln across the river and pointed to a spot on the ground. "This is perfect," he said to Metzler, who promptly marked the spot by driving a tent stake through the rain-soaked grass. The following day, the Army Corps of Engineers found Walton to be less than six inches off the actual axis.

Jackie returned home and crafted the particulars of the funeral. Longtime friend and designer of the Rose Garden at the White House[382] Bunny Mellon arrived. Jackie placed her in charge of the Arlington flowers with instructions to display them, but away from the burial site. General Clifton then approached Jackie with a request from the State Department to withdraw the invitation to the Black Watch to participate in the procession. Argentina had offered to send musicians and had been denied, and other countries would do the same. The thought was that if all could not be accommodated, none should be. Jackie simply looked at Clifton and said, "Jack loved bagpipes," ending the discussion. Shriver came to her asking her to rethink her choice of Bishop Philip Hannan to deliver the homily at the funeral mass. Hannan was only an auxiliary bishop, and the church hierarchy would call for an archbishop to perform this function. "Just say I'm hysterical," she told Sarge. "It has to be [383] Hannan."[384]

Next came the branches of government. The next day the president would leave the White House for the final time. A horse-drawn caisson would bear him to the Capitol Building, where he would lie in state as the American people paid their respects. Remembering Jack's affection for Senator Mike Mansfield, Democratic majority leader, she told Shriver she wanted him to deliver the eulogy at the Rotunda. Yet another firestorm ensued, as this would violate protocol. First, the Rotunda was the home of the House of Representatives, thus the domain of the Speaker of the House. Second, the president pro tempore of the Senate, its ranking member, should speak, not the majority leader. Finally, of course, what of the Supreme Court? They should be represented as well. Shriver felt like he was planning a political convention rather than the burial of the commander in chief. Compromises were made, and the Speaker of the House spoke, as did the chief justice. However, Mike Mansfield spoke first, and he received a call from Mrs. Kennedy specifically inviting him to do so. He delivered the eulogy.

Midnight had long passed when Jackie sent a message to Bobby to come see her. "I have to see Jack in the morning…I want to say goodbye to him, and I want to put something in his coffin."

"I'll come with you," he told her. "We'll go down there together."

Bobby left, and Jackie sat at her desk and began writing, pouring herself onto page after page after page. And when she was finished, she placed it in an envelope and sealed it.

The November sun returned on Sunday morning, and the family gathered for mass in the East Room. A horse-drawn caisson waited to march the president up Pennsylvania Avenue to the Capitol, where he would be eulogized and then lie in state. It was the people's turn to pay their last respects.

Jackie made her first public appearance since the glimpse America caught of her upon the return of Jack's body to Washington on Friday night. Her children—Caroline, who would turn six in four days, and John, who would be three the next day—accompanied her.

Mass ended, and Jackie went upstairs to the family quarters. Caroline and John were dressed and ready to journey with her to the Capitol. "You must write a letter to daddy," she said, handing Caroline a piece of her blue stationery, "and tell him how much you love him."

John, too little to write, was told to draw, as neatly as he could, something to give to his father.

As Maud Shaw assisted the children, Jackie sat, her mind wandering. She wanted to give something to Jack, to bury a tangible piece of herself with him. She settled on two things that he loved and that meant the most to him, both gifts from her: a pair of gold cufflinks from their first year married and a scrimshaw carving of the presidential seal that she'd given him last Christmas. The cufflinks he wore at every opportunity possible, and the scrimshaw had sat on the corner of his Oval Office desk since the day she gave it to him.

When the children's letters were complete, she took them, sealed them, and carried them, along with the gifts, out of the room. Gerry Behn called Clint Hill. "Mrs. Kennedy wants to view the president," he told Hill, who immediately headed for the East Room. Jackie and Bobby Kennedy were standing in the doorway when he arrived.

"Bobby and I want to see the president," Jackie said.

"All right, Mrs. Kennedy. Let me make sure everything is okay." Hill and General McHugh went to work clearing the honor guards from the room.

As they began to file out Jackie whispered to Bobby, "They don't have to leave the room…Jack would be so lonely…if they were gone. Just have them turn around."

Bobby spoke to the lieutenant. "I don't want that," he said, and the lieutenant halted his men and ordered an about-face, which he himself also executed.

Hill and McHugh had reverently opened the lid of the coffin. At the sight of the president, Hill struggled to keep his composure while he and McHugh moved to flank the honor guard. Bobby and Jackie knelt at the open coffin. "It's not Jack, it's not Jack," [385] she thought and was ever grateful that there were no public viewings. Through anguished tears Jackie slid the letters, the cufflinks, and the scrimshaw into the coffin.

Bobby removed his PT 109 tie pin and, looking at Jackie, offered, "He should have this, shouldn't he?" She nodded and whispered yes, and then Bobby reached into his pocket and removed an engraved silver rosary that his wife, Ethel, had given him for a wedding present. He placed it in his brother's coffin.

Jackie turned to Clint Hill. "Mr. Hill," she said, "will you get me scissors?" [386] Hill retrieved scissors from the office across the hall and watched as Jackie clipped locks from Jack's hair. Bobby then gently closed the lid of the coffin, and he and Jackie, both near inconsolable, turned away. Hill stayed close, fearing she might faint as she clung to Bobby as they left the room.

"The sight and sound of their agony is something I will never forget," Hill wrote fifty years later.[387]

Shattered in anguish and crushed with grief, Jackie had little time to allow it. The Marine Corps Band was assembled on the White House lawn, and the caisson was moving into place. In twenty minutes she would walk out the front door of the White House, a child in each hand, to follow their father's flag-draped coffin.

The casket team wheeled the coffin into the White House entrance hall. A day short of three years old, John had two passions in life. One was helicopters and the other soldiering. Enamored at the contingent of soldiers in full dress uniform, he intently watched as they delicately moved his father's coffin toward the door. "Mummy," he asked, "what are they doing?"

"They're taking daddy out," came her gentle reply.

Not satisfied he wanted to know, "Why do they do it so funny... so slow?"

"Because they're so sad," Jackie whispered.[388]

It was a silent forty-one-minute ride up Pennsylvania Avenue, as Jackie and the children shared a ride with Bobby and President and Mrs. Johnson to the foot of the thirty-six Capitol steps. Thousands lined the avenue, and thousands more followed behind the cortege. The casket team now faced their most daunting challenge: carrying the near one-thousand-pound coffin of their commander in chief up those thirty-six steps. Jackie emerged from the car with Caroline and John in tow. Hand in hand the three walked to the base of the steps to await the removal of the coffin from the caisson. First, however, the United States Marine Corps band paid tribute to their chief. In a slower than normal tempo, they played "Hail to the Chief."

Jackie was overcome. Bowing her head, her shoulders shook and her body was racked with sobs, yet within seconds she gathered herself and, with the singularity of purpose she'd shown since Dallas, her head lifted and she stood erect as the band finished their tribute. Jack's sisters, Jean, Eunice, and

Under the watchful eye of his wife and children, Jack's coffin is placed on the caisson for the trip up Pennsylvania Avenue to lie in state in the Capitol Rotunda. Behind Jackie are Jack's brother Bobby, sister Eunice Shriver, brothers-in law Stephen Smith and Sargent Shriver, and President Johnson.

Patricia, were also struck deeply by the band's slowed version of a song they'd come to love. Patricia was inspired by Jackie's composure. Her eyes never left her. "If Jackie can do it," she told herself, "so can I."[389] Jackie waited until the coffin was halfway up the steps and then, with children in hand, followed her husband. The powerful men of the nation fell in step behind her.

The ceremony inside lasted only fourteen minutes as Senator Mike Mansfield, Speaker John McCormack, and Chief Justice Earl Warren delivered eulogies. Mansfield spoke first, and his words wove the theme of Jackie's horror in Parkland Hospital. "There was a husband who asked much and gave much, and out of the giving and the asking wove with a woman what could not be broken in life, and in a moment it was no more. And so she took a ring from her finger and placed it in his hands, and kissed him and closed the lid of a coffin." Finishing, Mansfield walked to Jackie and handed her his manuscript.

"You anticipate me," she said to him. "How did you know I wanted it?"

"I didn't," came the senator's reply. "I just wanted you to have it."

In the majesty of the Capitol Rotunda, the eulogies came to an end. President Johnson, on behalf of a bereaved nation, laid a wreath at the bier. Jackie, not quite ready to leave, bent and whispered in her daughter's ear. Then, with Caroline, she walked toward the coffin. The only sound was Jackie's heels as she led her daughter to kneel at her daddy's bier. Caroline watched her every move, emulating each one. Jackie knelt next to the coffin, took the flag in both hands, and placed a kiss upon it. Caroline reached beneath the flag, getting as close to her dad as possible, and laid her hand on the coffin. Audible cries rose from the gathered, and tears fell down the faces of the mighty of the nation. Senators, congressmen, generals, and agents alike united in a heart-wrenching moment that illustrated the true measure of what was lost.

Jackie stood, taking Caroline's hand, and retraced her steps toward the exit. John rejoined his mother and sister as they walked down the thirty-six steps to the car and the trip home to the White House. Eyeing Lady Bird Johnson, Jackie approached her. "Lady Bird," Jackie said to the new first lady, "you must come to see me soon and we'll talk about you moving in." Completely caught off guard, Lady Bird let Jackie know she could "wait till whenever you're ready."

"Any time after tomorrow," came Jackie's retort. "I won't have anything to do after that."

Bedlam reigned in the White House as family and intimates arrived. Sleeping arrangements took on the tenor of an impromptu slumber party, with various people moving from one room to another, and cots were rolled in and out. The arrangements were fluid based on who had arrived when.

With the details for Monday's funeral far from finalized, Shriver, Ralph Dungan, Walton, General McHugh, and Tish Baldridge gathered to finalize them. The murder of the accused assassin found the Secret Service revisiting the prudence of President Johnson walking behind Jackie. Initially he had agreed and removed himself from the walking list, but he rejoined after Lady Bird told him he should do it.

The enormity of the task, coupled with the enormity of the loss, was exacerbated by the fact that all parties involved were now into the third day with little, if any, sleep. Sadness and exhaustion combined with the pressure of executing the chief's funeral with the solemnity, dignity, and majesty it warranted resulted in frayed nerves and quick tempers.

Jackie and Caroline say goodbye to Jack. "We're going to say goodbye to daddy, we're going to kiss him and tell him how much we love him and how much we'll always miss him," Jackie told Caroline before they approached the bier.

Jackie returned from the Rotunda and sealed herself off in her sitting room upstairs. She immediately placed calls to Mansfield, McCormack, and Warren to thank them for their words, leaving each man unable to speak. She was mindful of the urgency of funereal decisions, and she made them, bringing calm to the contentious decision makers. "Jackie had got things in control again," said Ralph Dungan.

With Bobby, Ethel, and Sarge, Jackie put together the details for the funeral mass. It was the selection of words that required the most thought, and for that Ted Sorensen (Jack's primary speech writer) and McGeorge Bundy were summoned for help. Jackie wanted a collection of Jack's words and Bible verses. Bobby opted for the beatitudes written by Matthew. "Blessed are the peacemakers" struck closest to Bobby's heart, as it would serve as a testament to President Kennedy's recent signing of the Nuclear Test Ban Treaty. In his mind, and the mind of many, this was his brother's greatest accomplishment.

Jackie, sitting on the couch between Sorensen and Bundy, shook her head no. She wanted something mournful. "What about Ecclesiastes?" she offered. "He loved it so." She went to her bookshelf and handed Sorensen her Bible. "Third chapter," she told him and sat back down.

"To everything there is a season, and a time for every purpose under heaven. A time to be born and a time to die," Sorensen read aloud. "This mightn't be wrong at all," he said upon completion.

Jackie later recalled, "It was so right that it just made shivers through your flesh."

Bundy and Sorensen were poring over Jack's words while Jackie sat apart from them, deeply lost in thought. Suddenly and seemingly from out of nowhere, she said, "And there's going to be an eternal flame."

Everybody stopped, and all heads turned to her looking "rather horrified." Sarge spoke. "We'll have to find out if there's one at the Tomb of the Unknown Soldier," he said. "Because if there is, we can't have one."

"I don't care if one's there," she replied, undaunted. "We're going to have it anyway."

Sarge placed a call to the Pentagon and to his surprise learned that there were only two eternal flames, one at the Arc de Triomphe in Paris (from where Jackie got the idea) and one at Gettysburg. And with that he ordered one be installed, adding, "And fix it so she can light it."

Richard Goodwin took on the role of liaison between Jackie and the Pentagon in the installation of the single most powerful attribute to sustain the legacy of her husband. Jackie was moved by the fact that the lights "on the top of the hill" at Arlington (Custis Lee mansion) were the first thing Caroline recognized as part of the Washington landscape. Now the flame burning at Jack's grave would also mark the landscape of the nation's capital. It would be an eternal reminder intoning the words of his inaugural address that "the torch had been passed to a new generation of Americans… And the glow from that fire can truly light the world. And so my fellow Americans, ask not what your country can do for you, ask what you can do for your country."

Jackie's resolute strength, courage, and determination ensured her objective: countless generations to follow would not forget her husband. "It came out right," McGeorge Bundy would later write, "as did just about everything that Jackie touched those days…And she touched everything."[390]

At 9:00 p.m. Jackie and Bobby returned to the Capitol. The line of people stretched for three miles and was eight, ten, and twelve across. Some estimates said that 500,000 people would pass through the Rotunda, and thousands more would wait in line, full in the knowledge they would not get through in time to view the president's coffin. Bobby and Jackie knelt at the bier and prayed for a few minutes before Jackie rose, kissed the coffin, and genuflected. Leaving the Rotunda, a middle-aged redheaded woman recognized her coming toward her and burst into tears. As if greeting a friend or relative, Jackie walked to her, and the two hugged. No words were exchanged, only the comforting embrace. They reached the bottom of the steps, and Jackie eschewed the open car door.

"No, let's walk," she said to Bobby, and alone the pair strolled across the lawn, emerging on the street below. On the street a nun recognized the pair and extended her sympathies. "Thank you,"[391] said Jackie, and they moved on with the limousine close behind. For fifteen minutes Jackie and Bobby Kennedy walked the streets of Washington, D.C., among the hundreds of thousands who had come to mourn President Kennedy. As more and more people began to recognize them, they retreated to the car and rode home to the White House.

Tomorrow, Jack would be laid to rest.

It was a clear, crisp morning, the sky a brilliant blue, the deep, clear blue that always accompanies the onset of winter as the chill sweeps away the remnants of heavy summer air. In the upstairs dining room Maud Shaw and Caroline sang happy birthday to the girl's little brother, John, and he opened two gifts: a helicopter from Caroline and a copy of Beatrix Potter's *Peter Rabbit* from Miss Shaw. Following breakfast, Miss Shaw put them back into their blue suits and red shoes, taking Caroline downstairs and leaving John with Dave Powers. Jackie prepared herself to say goodbye to Jack.

On the first floor the logistics of protocol were a complex tribulation, while the security concerns were a full-fledged nightmare. Jackie's insistence to walk behind Jack's coffin struck fear in the hearts of formidable, gathered security forces. The Pentagon and D.C. police had over four thousand armed men dispersed among the mourners. The White House detail walked in the procession along with 64 CIA men, 40 FBI agents, and 250 members of the State Department security team.

It is not an exaggeration to say that a near panic was brewing. A groundswell was growing to stop the walking. Cabinet members, the Secret Service, and staffers wanted it stopped, and the director of the FBI, J. Edgar

Hoover, officially weighed in, stating that he "advised against" the march. Some agents, on an individual basis, were trying to convince some walkers to get into automobiles. Only one person truly possessed the power to call off the march, and she was steadfast and resolute. Gerry Behn, in a last-ditch attempt to stop it, again approached Clint Hill and asked if he thought Mrs. Kennedy would ride in a limousine with President Johnson. "You can try if you want to," Hill said, shaking his head. "She really wants to walk all the way, and if it wasn't for the old men, she would."[392]

Returning to the Capitol steps, Jackie, Bobby, and Teddy Kennedy emerged from the caravan's lead car at 10:40 a.m. Wanting just one more moment of privacy, Bobby suggested the three of them go into the Rotunda. For ten minutes they knelt at Jack's bier, then they arose and left, and the casket team moved into place.

Jack's last ride down Pennsylvania Avenue took nearly thirty minutes, as the cortege returned to the White House where the world's mighty assembled, waiting for Jackie to lead them. The Marine Corps Band, for which Jack had a special affinity, led the caisson. He had once quipped to Jackie in his patented wry, self-deprecating manner that the Marine Band were "the only troops I command...the rest belong to McNamara."[393] This was yet another unknown small detail, not lost on Jackie, that brought a deeply personal touch to the majesty of the moment.

Exiting the vehicle in the White House drive, Jackie was taken aback at the assemblage. In all of her conversations regarding the security dangers of this endeavor, she had given little thought to who would fall in behind her and really didn't think anyone would. Scanning the faces, her eyes met the eyes of General de Gaulle. Looking from behind the black veil that covered her face, she nodded. And she remembered, "He was sort of nodding and bowing his head, his face just stricken."[394] It was a tribute to her from the French leader, whom she once said "was my hero when I married Jack."[395] Jackie was touched by de Gaulle's presence at the funeral.

"You know, he realized who Jack was, and that's why he came...He didn't need to do that." [396] What Jackie did not know was that upon learning of Jack's assassination he, a victim of several attempts himself, was one of the first heads of state to contact the United States State Department to say he would attend the funeral.

With the church bells ringing, Jackie started to walk. Bobby moved in on her right side, taking her hand, and Ted stepped to her left. Beginning their march out the driveway towards Pennsylvania Avenue, the shrill sound of the Black Watch's bagpipes could be heard. Jackie's eyes filled with tears, and she teetered. Then came the sounds of muffled drums, and she found herself, straightened, dropped Bobby's hand, and stepped forward. With her head erect and the wind lightly pressing her black veil to her face, she

Jackie, flanked by her brothers-in-law, Robert (l) and Ted (r), follows Jack's coffin as they leave the White House on their one mile walk to St. Matthew's Cathedral for the president's funeral.

walked, cognizant only of the voices of Bobby and Ted while the millions of people who lined Washington's streets saw only her.

Thirty-nine minutes was all it took from the time the caisson rolled out the front gate until the military honor guard wheeled the president's coffin down the center aisle of St. Matthew's Cathedral. In that time frame, Jacqueline Kennedy received worldwide veneration that few have known. Across the Atlantic, Lady Jeanne Campbell wrote in London's *Evening Standard* that Jackie had "given the American people, from this day on, the one thing they've always lacked, majesty."[397] On the other side of the world Australians touted "Mrs. Kennedy's Courage."[398] North of the border, they thought her "sustained by some unknown inner strength…she walked purposeful and erect, never faltering."[399] And back in Great Britain, Hella Pick mirrored Campbell's sentiment in London's *Guardian*: "The steadfast bearing and dignity of Jacqueline Kennedy…the dignified display of love and sorrow, her luminous beauty have been the universal admiration of the American nation."[400]

Across the American nation, cities and towns, hamlets and villages, echoed with their own expressions of respect and admiration. Pittsburgh saw how "she met unspeakable tragedy with serenity and heroic poise,"[401] and Boston found Jackie "had given his death a grandeur an assassin's bullet tried to take away."[402] Her beloved Newport noted how "bravely she walked…a black veil covered her face," leading "one of the greatest assemblages of world statesmen ever seen."[403] "Jacqueline Kennedy, who captured the heart of the American people as first lady," New York declared, "won new respect today for her courage and dignity as a woman." The paper added, "Few women could meet the standards Jacqueline Kennedy set for herself in her bereavement."[404] Los Angeles "marveled at the strength and spirit of Jacqueline Kennedy…a queenly and sorrowful figure."[405] In Tampa, where Jack had visited days before Dallas, they declared her "Majestic in

Her Sorrow…ever erect, never faltering…her head high even in grief… she enthralled the world with her emotional composure." [406] In the fiftieth state, Hawaii, Senator Daniel Inouye said, "Seeing her I couldn't help but be inspired. She is the pride of American womanhood." Congressman Spark Matsunaga added, "In Jacqueline Kennedy, American womanhood—long epitomized by the pioneer's wife—has blossomed into full bloom for the entire world to hold in admiration." [407]

The Kansas heartland was effusive with praise. "None can know… the yearning misery…of the long dark hours…A courageous American woman…composed and dignified…accepting with fortitude the inevitable. It is said that in times of tragedy and great sorrow, some have the capacity to rise to the heights. This, we believe, certainly applies to Jacqueline Kennedy. In the eyes of her countrymen, her darkest hour, has been her finest." [408] In Washington, watching the cortege from a fourth-floor window, *National Geographic* magazine editor Melville Grosvenor observed, "Jacqueline Kennedy walked with a poise and grace that words cannot convey…as regal as any emperor, queen or prince who followed her." [409]

Perhaps the most poignant praise came from the most unexpected source: the editorial pages of the *Montgomery, Alabama Journal*. This was Alabama, "with its vicious racists, with its governor having his lips dripping with the words of interposition and nullification," [410] who said, "Segregation today, segregation tomorrow, segregation forever."

On Friday, as Jackie Kennedy was sitting outside Parkland Hospital's trauma room one, awaiting a coffin for her husband, students at Montgomery's Lanier High School cheered and applauded the news of the president's death. In another section of the city, an automobile with anti-Kennedy adornments and cheering passengers drove about blaring its horn.

The editorial board of the *Alabama Journal* was not enamored with the politics of the Kennedy administration nor the lifestyle of its first lady.

However, watching Jackie publicly carry the weight of her seemingly insurmountable burden revealed to them qualities within her they never expected to see. Transformed and moved, they chose to speak, and they spoke in recognition of the agony of her loss of both Patrick and Jack:

> Comment on President Kennedy's death cannot be closed without paying tribute to the regal comportment of Jacqueline Kennedy, who has displayed qualities few of us knew were in her. As first lady she seemed most interested in the glittering cosmopolite...exciting life that fate had handed her...Proving once again that it's an error to judge human character by superficialities. Mrs. Kennedy first demonstrated her qualities of faith and strength on the death of her prematurely born child a short time ago. Few women have to endure another grief so soon. The nobility and grace of her bearing of the ordeal, which has not ended for her and never will be, was all the more admirable because she was at her husband's side when he was taken from her so violently...she was there when an assassin's bullet shattered her husband's head, in a moment of smiling triumphant reception by the people of Dallas. She tried to hold life in him when seeing the grievous wound, she must have known that their time together had ended. Through it all she bore up with remarkable composure, sustained we must assume, by a faith stronger than death. To Jacqueline Kennedy, whom many of us have misjudged, a salute. She has set an example for the nation which it will never forget.[411]

On the steps of St. Matthew's Cathedral, Richard Cardinal Cushing stood waiting for his president, his friend, his widow. Glimpsing the flag-draped coffin brought tears to the vicar's eyes, which he wiped with a trembling hand. Jackie spotted him and was struck by how "enormous" he appeared.[412] The caisson stopped in front of the church, and Agent Foster, who rode with the children directly behind her, delivered them to her. Taking them by their hands, Jackie stood while "Hail to the Chief" again was played. The hymn "Prayer for the Dead" followed, after which Cushing opened his arms to Jackie and then the children. He kissed her, and in her words, he "shepherded me in" to the church.

Sitting in the first pew, with Caroline at her side (Foster had once again rescued John), Jackie sat as the ritual of her lifetime unfolded. For ten years she and Jack had shared Sunday mass together in Hyannis Port, Washington, Virginia, and of course, at St. Mary's in Newport.

Cardinal Cushing led the procession down the aisle, and as he donned the vestments for the mass, the casket team wheeled Jack's coffin into place beside Jackie. From the balcony, as it had a decade before while she knelt with Jack at the altar of St. Mary's, came the voice of Luigi Vena singing the words of the "Ave Maria." The song washed over her. All of it washed over her—her wedding day, Arabella, Patrick, Dallas. She had almost lost him twice in the nascent years of her marriage, and now he lay in a coffin next to her, forever gone. Cushing, dressed in the black vestments of the funeral mass, began the prayers in the Latin of the Roman Catholic ritual.

Jackie, veiled in black, hung her head, and the tears came. The weight crashed down upon her, and she was now crying uncontrollably, her shoulders shaking with spasmodic sobs. She had made but one seating request, and that was to make sure that Clint Hill sat behind her. Hill reached into his pocket and handed her a handkerchief, and the sobs still came, emptying her soul. And then, a comforting squeeze clasped her hand, as Caroline sought to ease her mother's anguish. The spasms subsided, and her composure, which had defined her, returned.

The mass she had carefully crafted was elegant in its simplicity. The only voices heard were the nasal, gravelly intonations of Cardinal Cushing and the smooth recitations of Bishop Hannan. Hannan read from five Scripture passages, most of which the president had used in speeches. And, of course, he read from Ecclesiastes. He closed with selections from Jack's inaugural address, ending with the words: "Let us go forth to lead the land we love, asking His blessing and His help but knowing that here on earth, God's work must truly be our own."

With the mass itself officially ended, the cardinal made his way to the bier. Intoning in Latin as he had done throughout, he began the parting prayers. Finishing the first segment, he paused. Looking toward the heavens, he sighed. "May the angels, dear Jack," he prayed, "lead you into paradise. May the martyrs," and he again paused as his mind searched for the English translation to the Latin words he'd uttered countless times, "receive you at your coming." Then he finished, "May the spirit of God, embrace you, and mayest thou, with all those who made the supreme sacrifice of dying for others, receive eternal peace. Amen."[413]

Jackie could see the tears in his eyes, and as he made his way to the side of the altar to change from the black vestments of the mass, she thought to herself, "He was the one person who had the right to call him 'dear Jack.'"[414] For "he [Jack] was devoted to Cushing and Cushing was devoted to him."[415] The pathos of the moment struck her and, once again, so did the tears. Looking up at her mother's tear-stained face, Caroline clasped her hand. "You'll be all right, Mummy. Don't cry. I'll take care of you."[416]

While changing vestments and fighting back his own tears, Cushing noticed Caroline comforting her mother. Now adorned in the royal, scarlet red of his station, he stepped from the altar and went right to Jackie. Taking her hand, she rested her cheek against his. "I'll never forget you calling him 'dear

Jack,'"[417] she said, still seeking her composure. He squeezed her hand tightly and then reached for Caroline. Taking the girl's hand, the sixty-eight-year-old prelate drew her closer and stretched forward to peck her cheek. Cardinal Cushing had known Jack for two decades. He had married him, baptized his daughter, prayed at his inauguration, and buried his son. And now he led his coffin down the aisle of St. Matthew's. Agent Foster returned with John, and with the children again in hand, Jackie followed Cardinal Cushing and Jack's coffin as outside "Hail to the Chief" played for Jack one last time.

They followed the casket down the stairs, and when they reached the bottom, Cardinal Cushing sprinkled holy water on it before placing a kiss on the flag. Lieutenant Bird's team then gently returned the president to the caisson for his final trip to Arlington. The band was playing "Holy God We Praise Thy Name," and as the honor guard fastened the straps over the coffin, Jackie bent down and whispered in John's ear. "John," she said, "you can salute daddy now and say goodbye to him."

John loved to play soldier with his dad, and a part of that play was saluting. It had always been playful, and Jackie once described John's salute as "sort of droopy."[418] But not on this day. Something had touched the little boy, who was today three years old. He stepped away from his mom, and perfectly cocking his right elbow, he brought his hand over his right eye to where it just touched his hair. His left arm was rigid at his side, and his red shoes stood perfectly side by side. With his shoulders squared and his chin in, he held his salute for six seconds.

The long line of black limousines began to arrive. Mr. Foster took Caroline and John back to their car to return them to the White House. Jackie got into the first car and waited to begin Jack's final journey, past the Lincoln Memorial and over Memorial Bridge to Arlington. Presidents Truman and Eisenhower came to Jackie, paying their respects. In every direction stood rows and rows of people, thousands standing in eerie silence under a palpable pall of profound sadness. Off in the distance came the sound of muffled drums, which grew continually closer, continually louder, and then the call to arms beckoned the silver gray horses to action and the final march began.

The only audible sounds came from the cortege: the band's cutting melodies, the incessant beat of the drums, and in the sporadic interims where they fell silent, there was the clip-clopping echo of the silver gray horses carrying Jack to his final rest. As it crossed the bridge to Arlington, CBS commentator Roger Mudd whispered into his microphone, "A scene of great majesty, serenity and grief."

Emerging from the car, Jackie took Bobby's hand as they, along with Teddy, led the family to the graveside. The national anthem played as the casket team began their final removal of Jack's coffin from the caisson. The strains of the bagpipes from the U.S. Air Force cascaded over the Arlington green while Lieutenant Bird's casket team bore their commander to his

Jackie bent down and whispered in John's ear that it was time to salute daddy. The three-year-old boy stepped away from his mom and saluted. His salute, usually droopy, was strong and firm and he held it for six seconds while 65,000,000 Americans gasped.

final rest. As they lay the coffin on the grave, a combination of Air Force and Navy jets roared across the sky—fifty of them in all, representing the fifty American states, in sixteen formations of three with the last formation missing a plane, signifying the loss of the leader.

Jackie took her place as the casket team lifted the flag and was now holding it tautly over the coffin. From above came an approaching high-pitched scream as Air Force I flew over, dipping its wing in a final salute to President Kennedy. The voice of Cardinal Cushing was once again heard as he blessed the grave of his personal friend. Calling him, "Our beloved Jack Kennedy, thirty-fifth President of the United States," he asked of God "that his soul may rejoice in thee."[419] The guns of salute began to fire.

Jackie never wavered. She stood erect, head high, shoulders back, the epitome of posture, unflinching as the thunderous cannons echoed down the hillside of Arlington. Her hands were folded before her, and her eyes never left the coffin. When the cannons fell silent, Jackie and Bobby moved to the head of the coffin. Teddy stood right behind them. Three short rifle reports followed, and then the bugler played taps. After a slight pause, the Marine Band, Jack's troops, began the "Navy Hymn."

Throughout it all the honor guard, the men who had been with Jack every step of the way since he'd left Bethesda Hospital on early Saturday morning, did not move. They stood at attention, their hands tightly holding the flag. Now came the moment for their final tribute. With immaculate precision the flag was folded, each pair of hands working in unison, until it reached the foot of the casket. Sergeant James Feldor, after making the final tuck on the trifold flag, handed it across the coffin, and it was passed breast to breast back to the head of the grave. Specialist Four Douglas Mayfield, with trembling lip and tear-filled eyes, handed it to Arlington superintendent John Metzler and saluted. Metzler, himself struggling for composure, moved toward the widowed first lady. His words were interrupted by his emotion, but he managed to deliver a deep and meaningful condolence. "Mrs. Kennedy," he said, "this flag is presented to you in the name of a most mournful nation." Holding it out to her he could only whisper, "Please take it." [420]

Without saying a word, Jackie clutched the flag to her breast and then moved to the head of the grave.

The time had come to light the flame, and for the final time Richard Cardinal Cushing was called upon for a blessing. "Our help is in the name of the Lord who made heaven and earth," he began, and from there on, he improvised as the Catholic Church had no formal ritual for the blessing of a flame. The final intonation of Boston's craggy archangel was a reference to Jack as "the wonderful man we bury here today." [421]

Stepping to Mrs. Kennedy, Major Converse of the Army Corps of Engineers handed her the burning wick. "This is the saddest moment of my life," [422] he said as he led her to the symmetrically piled evergreens at the head of the coffin. She touched the flame to the tip of the torch, and it instantaneously breathed fire. She turned to Bobby, handing him the wick, which he ceremoniously placed into the fire. Teddy followed and handed it back to the major, who extinguished it. The ceremony was over. The majestic farewell to the fallen president now, like Lincoln, belonged to the ages.

Jackie's left hand clutched Jack's flag, and she held it close to her breast. Bobby reached for her free hand, and together they walked past Jack's coffin down the Arlington slope. Twice they paused, as Jackie comforted Maxwell Taylor and thanked Bishop Hannan for the "splendid" [423] eulogy. She then parted the sea of humanity comprising kings and queens, generals, and prime ministers, emperors and heads of state, all giving way to the young widow, who "during those four endless days in 1963...held us together as a family and a country. In large part because of her we could grieve and then go on." [424]

They were about to enter the car when Jackie noticed Lady Bird Johnson coming toward her. With her was Johnny Connally, the seventeen-year-old son of the Texas governor who was recuperating in Parkland Hospital. He carried with him a letter from his mother that he wanted to deliver. Jackie graciously accepted the letter and inquired about his father's condition.

Coming over the bridge, Bobby asked the driver to stop the car for a moment, and the three of them peered out the window through the columns at the statue of the sitting Lincoln, his face furrowed and care-worn by the ravages of war. The widow and the brothers sat silently together, thinking thoughts known only to themselves and their God.

Nearly 100 percent of Americans spent some portion of their weekend watching the funeral ceremonies of their president. Virtually every American had witnessed some measure of Jackie's endless, elegant display of fortitude. Her day, however, was far from over, as she would receive, at the White House, all the representatives of the countries of the world who had traveled to pay their respects to Jack.

Upstairs in the White House, her family was gathered hovering around a television, watching the local news with replay after replay of the funeral. Present were Kennedys, Shrivers, Smiths, Lawfords, Radziwills, and Auchinclosses. And, of course, the Irish mafia. Jackie entered and made her rounds, speaking to each individually, thanking them for all they had done and bringing comfort.

Downstairs the dignitaries were gathered, and Jackie asked that all the family take turns greeting them in the Red Room. Teddy, along with his sisters Eunice, Pat, and Jean, headed downstairs. Jackie, meanwhile, placed a call to Evelyn Lincoln, asking if she could come upstairs and keep company with Rose Kennedy. "I have to comb my hair for all these dignitaries," she said, leaving Jack's secretary of twelve years to wonder to herself, "How do you do it?"[425]

Jackie asked Angier Biddle Duke if he could arrange for Ethiopian emperor Haile Selassie, French president Charles de Gaulle, Ireland's president Eamon de Valera, and Prince Philip of Great Britain to visit her in the upstairs living quarters.

First came the emperor, whom Jackie and Jack had greeted together at Washington's Union Station just six weeks prior. It was Jackie's first public appearance since the death of Patrick, and in an ironic twist, she presented to Selassie's granddaughter a bouquet of red roses welcoming her to America. They spoke in French, for Selassie's English was limited, and after their visit Jackie fetched the children from across the hall. They were enraptured by him during his October visit. "He was their hero," Jackie remembered, and as the children paused, tentatively looking through the door, Jackie said, "Look, John, he's such a brave soldier. That's why he has all those medals." John climbed on his lap to inspect those medals, while Caroline ran to get the doll he had given her in October.

"You will be a brave warrior," said the emperor to John, in his best English. "Like your father."

Caroline returned, and now they were sharing his lap, showing him the ivory carvings he had given them. Jackie noted that it seemed as if a transcendental bond existed between this ancient, bearded warrior, bedecked in military splendor, and her children. For twenty minutes they sat together, enthralled with him. "He had this thing of love," Jackie would later recall. "They showed him their little presents, and they were so happy, just staring at him and worshipping." [426]

The warmth of this gentle encounter ended, and President de Gaulle was next to enter. They had not seen each other since the splendor of Paris in June 1961, and now he was here to pay his respects to her and to her husband. On this day she would meet him as an equal with a singular purpose in mind.

McGeorge Bundy noted that "she received him like a queen," [427] in what was essentially a diplomatic meeting. Sitting across from him beneath the mantle of her fireplace, she spoke to her point. Jackie was aware that some acrimony had stirred within the French diplomatic corps regarding the scuttling of a missile program. She also knew that de Gaulle would be meeting that very night with President Johnson, and she wanted to convey to de Gaulle a simple message. She wanted to impart to him Jack's understanding of each leader's desire and need to do, in their hearts and minds, what was right for their people. However, bitterness had emerged among these allies, and she called to de Gaulle's mind that his ambassador, Hervé Alphand, was among the embittered. More than anything she wanted him to know that "Jack was never bitter."[428] It was a simple message delivered from the heart of the woman who had beguiled him in France.

The meeting ended, and she escorted the president across the hall to the waiting elevator. They passed a chest de Gaulle had gifted to her and her husband, on which sat a vase filled with daisies. Plucking one she handed it to him. "I want you to take this as a last remembrance of the president,"[429] she said. The French president rode the elevator holding the American daisy in memory of the fallen American president.

Dining with Ambassador and Madame Alphand before meeting with President Johnson, de Gaulle was quiet throughout most of the meal, perhaps ruminating on his own thoughts and images of the past few dark and endless days. Roused from his inner thoughts, he turned to Nicole Alphand. "Madame," he said wearily, showing her the daisy. "This is the last souvenir I shall have of President Kennedy. She asked me to keep it, and I shall keep it always." Gently he returned it to his pocket, and through a sigh he said, "She gave an example to the whole world on how to behave."[430]

Bobby brought Eamon de Valera to her, the Irish president who, when Jack was only two years old, drew over sixty thousand people to hear him speak of Irish independence at Boston's Fenway Park. Just five months earlier he had welcomed President Kennedy to his country on a journey that touched Jack's soul. He brought with him a letter from his wife, whom Jack had so enjoyed during his visit. They spoke of everything Irish: of Jack's visit, of de Valera's wife, of legends of the Emerald Isle, of its rich poetry, and particularly of a Gerald Griffin poem that was a tribute to the land, its people, and their struggles. Mrs. de Valera had recited it for Jack when he visited. Jack was so moved by it, he had memorized it himself.

The poignancy of the memories overwhelmed them, and with tears flowing down both their faces, Bobby escorted de Valera out through what had been Jack's adjoining bedroom. Jackie, choking back sobs, opened the doorway to the hall to find Prince Philip. He was squatting on the floor with John, and they were laughing. Gathering herself, Jackie curtsied. Standing, the prince told Jackie how much John reminded him of his son, Charles, when he was his age. "John," she said, "did you make your bow to the prince?"

"I did," came the boy's reply without looking up, invoking laughter and easing the moment. Lee and Biddle Duke joined them, and with Jackie's prodding look, the prince advised her on the reception downstairs. "I'd advise you to have the line," he told her. "It's really quick and it gets it done."[431]

Angier Biddle Duke remembered that in June 1961, aboard Air Force I on their way to London and dinner with the queen, Jackie had summoned him. She inquired if protocol called for her to "curtsey" before Queen Elizabeth. Duke's response was swift and emphatic: "The wife of a chief of state never curtsies to anyone."[432] Duke was in the hallway when Jackie found the prince playing with John on the floor. Following her curtsey, she had stepped aside, letting the prince into the room ahead of her. Glancing at Duke with a forlorn smile, she said to him, "Angie, I'm no longer the wife of a chief of state." Recalling that story twenty-five years later, fighting tears and in a voice choked with emotion, Duke said, "I promise you, I nearly broke down."[433]

All present in the Red Room were surprised to learn that the widow had joined them. Taking the advice of Prince Philip, Jackie took her position to receive her guests. Teddy was on her right and Angie on her left, with General McHugh nearby, ready to lend a hand.

Disconsolate and forlorn, she greeted them all. One by one they paused, and she shook their hands, exchanging words of gratitude and appreciation. Emotionally exhausted and physically drained, she carried out her duty to the last and still managed to bring comfort to those who came to comfort her.

Ludwig Erhard, only a month removed from his election as chancellor of West Germany, was to have been the guest of the President and Mrs. Kennedy this very evening. Joining them was to be Werner Von Braun, the German-born rocket genius whom Jack had visited at Cape Canaveral a mere week ago. He came to her, and she shook his hand. Holding him in the line, she whispered to him, "I was looking forward to a state dinner with you this very evening. I had ordered German wine and German music...under other circumstances we would be dining together tonight, with German music playing in this very house." Too moved to speak, Erhard simply nodded before making his way out, visibly moved by their exchange.

Looking down the line Jackie could see Anastas Mikoyan, the first deputy of Nikita Khrushchev and the second most powerful man in the Soviet Union. The crusty old Bolshevik had fought in the Russian Revolution, survived Stalin's purges, and now served as Khrushchev's right-hand man. It was his sixty-eighth birthday, and as he waited on line to see the president's widow, his distress was obvious to even a casual observer. Trembling when he approached her, it was clear he was at a loss. Jackie reached for his hand and, holding it, said, "Please tell Mr. Chairman President that I know he and my husband worked together for a peaceful world, now he and you must carry on my husband's work."[434] The interpreter delivered her message, and Mikoyan crumbled. Futilely he tried to blink away his tears but he could not stop them, and he buried his face in his hands and wept.

Last in line was Lleras Camargo, the former president of Colombia and the founder of the Organization of American States. Camargo held a special place in Jackie's heart for the hospitality he had shown her and Jack on a state visit in December 1961. "Her stay in the house of the President, the state dinner that they gave at the Presidential Palace, the sense of the past—all of this gave her ideas about the maintenance and restoration of the White House."[435] She had once said to Jack that she believed Camargo to be the "greatest statesman I've ever met." Standing in front of her, both of them struggled for composure. With words that threatened to choke her, she told him that visiting his country was the best trip abroad she and the president had taken. The two of them began to weep, and Jackie said, "Please don't let them forget Jack."[436]

As she was leaving the room, Jackie beckoned to Clint Hill. "I may want to go back to Arlington later," she whispered to him. "I'll call you and let you know."

"Of course," Hill responded, adding, "I hate to bring this up, but I told Provi I'd remind you. Have you thought about doing anything for John's birthday?"

"Oh Mr. Hill, you never forget anything," she answered. "That's what we're going to do now. Everyone's upstairs and we're going to have a little celebration."[437]

Duke escorted her upstairs on the elevator. Words would not come to either of them for all they had left were tears. He was due at Lyndon Johnson's reception for the same individuals who had just paid Mrs. Kennedy their respects. Exiting, they stood in the hall, and Angie kissed her on both cheeks. She wept. In the elevator going back downstairs, the day overtook him and he, too, wept uncontrollably.

Jackie loved the King James Bible. She was inspired by it and took comfort from it. A devotee of poetry and herself a poet, she also drew from the prayers of her faith. She chose Ecclesiastes for Jack's funeral, and she, no doubt, took solace in one of her personal favorite passages: Saint Francis of Assisi's "Prayer for Peace," which reads in part:

Grant that I may not so much seek to be consoled as to console;
To be understood as to understand;
To be loved as to love;
For it is in giving that we receive;
It is in pardoning that we are pardoned;
And it is in dying that we are born into eternal life.

In the darkest days of her life, Jackie lived by these words. It had started in Dallas, when Henry Gonzalez fell to his knees before her in the Parkland Hospital emergency room, and had just concluded with two men, among the world's most powerful, who came seeking to console and were themselves consoled.

Composing herself, she walked through the hall. John and the bittersweet celebration of his third birthday were waiting. Glancing up she noticed a solitary figure. It was a young woman whom she did not recognize, and she immediately wondered who this woman was and, more importantly, how she got there. Lee emerged from the sitting room to introduce the young lady, who was Mary Ann Ryan. Through the efforts of a White House aide, Irish police, Pan Am airlines, and New York customs officials, Mary had arrived for the mass all the way from Dunganstown in County Wexford, Ireland. She was a cousin of Jack's, and they had met on Jack's trip in June, when Jack had put an arm around her and told her, "You know, you look like a Kennedy. You have that Irish smile."[438]

Her Irish smile was gone, replaced with the sadness of Jack's loss and the fact that she was now four thousand miles from home and knew nobody. Quickly understanding the young woman's plight and realizing there was still more giving to be done, Jackie excused herself. She went into Jack's bedroom and into his bureau drawer, returning with a set of his rosary beads for Mary and another religious artifact for her mother. Suddenly doors flew open, and in a matter of minutes the hall was filled with people of all ages. The family had converged, and they swept up Mary, who instantaneously was no longer alone. She was one of them.

In the sitting room the television was turned to NBC, airing the Johnson reception, when Willy Brandt appeared on the screen. Surprised, Jackie asked Bobby, "Why wasn't Willy Brandt in the line downstairs?" Brandt was the mayor of West Berlin, and as "only" a mayor, he was not high ranking enough to warrant an invitation to the reception following the funeral. Lee, who had been in Berlin with Jack, commented to Jackie how much she was impressed by Brandt. Jackie herself recalled the fondness with which Jack had praised him upon his return. Forty-eight hours after Jack's death, Brandt renamed the square where Kennedy had delivered his "Ich bin ein Berliner" speech John F. Kennedy Platz. It was a gesture that touched Jackie deeply.

"Well, I want to see him,"[439] she said. Joe West made a phone call, and ten minutes later Mayor Brandt was waiting in the oval room.

Bobby accompanied Jackie to the oval room, their emotional reserves gone, both completely exhausted. William Vanden Heuvel, an aide, said of Bobby, "I had never seen human pain expressed on someone's face that way. It was as if he had been mortally wounded and of course he had...because they were so close." And of Jackie he noted, "The country was held together... more than any other thing by Mrs. Kennedy. Her nobility, her strength, her courage...She just expressed it in a way that was eloquent without words; that one could be grief stricken so profoundly, yet understand that the responsibilities of life had to go on."[440] One more time they would need to draw strength from a reservoir that was virtually depleted.

They entered the room, and Brandt burst into tears. Consoling, Jackie asked about the renaming of the square. Acknowledging it while drying his eyes, Brandt told her it was not enough. He then asked permission to name a school after Jack. Jackie glanced at Bobby, who was now struggling to keep his composure. "Fine," was all he could say, and Jackie walked across the room to the window. Night had descended upon the city. The red beacon of the Washington Monument was flashing. Beyond, standing watch over the Potomac River, was the thirty-two-foot bronzed statue of Thomas Jefferson. The white dome of the Jefferson Memorial was now illuminated at night, by Jack's order.

"He can't have this view anymore," she said, still looking out the window, "but he can have John F. Kennedy Platz. Thank you for that." [441] Though her eyes filled with tears, they did not fall, and she did not falter. She turned to see that was not the case with her brother-in-law and the mayor, both of whom were openly weeping. *Grant that I may not so much seek to be consoled as to console.*

Dave Powers provided the high-water mark of the evening, and he did so by simply being Dave Powers. With him since the winter of 1946, Dave had been an invaluable political asset to Jack, and along the way he had become one of his closest and most trusted friends.

The evening was a cruel mix of a toddler's birthday party and Irish wake, and it was Powers who directed them both. To the delight of the children, he was the leader of their band, marching in cadence, around the entire suite. The aunts and uncles, moms and dads, were regaled with Dave's stories of his friend, bringing both laughter and tears. It was Jackie who suggested a sing-along with some of Jack's favorite songs. It was quickly suggested that there was no piano in the room, to which Dave replied, "We Irish don't need music to sing…The music's inside us," [442] and he broke into "That Old Gang of Mine." "Heart of My Heart" followed, and it proved too much for Bobby, who fled the room.

The children were put to bed, and the others dissipated to home or their respective rooms. It was not long before Bobby and Jackie found themselves alone. Five nights earlier, the two had sat in the very same room and talked for nearly an hour about the pending trip to Texas. Bobby had wondered how sure Jackie was that she was ready to absorb the rigors of this intense dip into the political pool of Jack's pending reelection campaign. There was a vibrant palpability to the surreal component surrounding them. However, the grotesque reality and regal splendor of the past three days were all too real. Jack was gone. And Bobby knew now and forevermore that there was nothing Jackie could not absorb, nothing she could not endure. He looked at her. "Shall we go see our friend?" he asked.[443]

Jackie called downstairs, waking Clint Hill, who had dozed off in his chair. "Yes, Mrs. Kennedy."

"Mr. Hill," she said, "Bobby and I want to go to Arlington. We want to see the flame."

"Certainly, Mrs. Kennedy," Hill replied. "I'll get the car."[444]

Hill had called ahead to Arlington, alerting them of the possibility of this visit. A second call was made to alert Superintendent Metzler that they were on their way.

On her way downstairs Jackie gathered a small bouquet of white lilies of the valley from a vase in the hallway. They retraced the path the cortege had followed just a few hours earlier, traveling over the Memorial Bridge, only this time a flame danced, flickering on the hillside below the Custis Lee Mansion. It was a moving, powerful moment. They left the vehicles, walking through the darkness among the cedar and oak trees, the flame flickering before them. A small white picket fence now surrounded the grave, and military caps were sprinkled throughout the flowers and the pines. The most conspicuous was a green beret from a member of the Special Forces team Jack had founded.

They knelt together, the widow and the president's brother, while the shimmering blue flame flirted with the nighttime November breeze. They prayed, heads bowed, and the Capitol clocks struck midnight. Jackie rose and placed her lilies next to the flame. Taking Bobby's hand, they walked through the small gate of the white fence and into the darkness, toward the lights of the nation's capital.

With silent, stoic grandeur Jackie Kennedy seared the soul of America. Bold and stouthearted, she walked out of Parkland Hospital, her hand gently resting on Jack's coffin. With an abiding conviction, she refused to change her blood-stained suit, facing the world wearing the scars of her personal horror. With dignified majesty she held the hands of her children while their father's flag-draped coffin left the White House for the final time. In a solemn woeful moment, standing at the foot of the thirty-six Capitol steps, again with her children in hand, she watched as their daddy's casket was removed from the caisson. The Marine Corps band played "Hail to the Chief," piercing her heart, and for seconds, only seconds, she lowered her head and wept, her shoulders shuddering in the spasm of her shattered soul. Standing stately in the Capitol Rotunda, she watched while her husband was placed on the catafalque, and with statuesque poise she listened while men of power eulogized him. With nurturing genteelness, she led Caroline to the bier, kneeling and gently kissing the flag that covered Jack's coffin before, hand in hand, mother and daughter exited down those same thirty-six steps. Elegant, erect, and valiant, she walked behind his horse-drawn caisson from the White House to St. Matthew's Cathedral. With a delicate tenderness she comforted her daughter, who during her daddy's funeral was overcome, crushed with the magnitude of her loss. With a soft, loving whisper she brought her three-year-old son to attention, and he saluted his daddy's flag-draped coffin. With a stirring grace she ignited the flame at his graveside, ensuring that her husband would eternally pass the torch to new generations of Americans. With courage and august nobility she walked, head held high behind a black veil, brave and polished, daunted not broken, but steadfast and determined that her husband would not be lost to history or forgotten by his people. The mighty of the world walked behind her, and with the bold conviction of every step, she stared down the face of evil, which took him from her.

Jacqueline Lee Bouvier Kennedy, the woman with no official government title or function, led the world to Arlington National Cemetery to lay to rest her "beloved Jack Kennedy, thirty-fifth president of the United States." She set out to mark his place in the history of his country. She became the symbol of American courage, grace, strength, resilience, and determination and thus marked her place as well.

# Epilogue

"I'll bring them all together now."

*Jacqueline Kennedy*

Jackie set out immediately to the task of cementing Jack's legacy, the anchors of which would be his final resting place in Arlington and the John F. Kennedy Library. In the weekend following Thanksgiving, just days after Jack's burial, Jackie met with author and presidential historian Theodore White. She told him of their habit of listening to records before bedtime, and Jack's favorite was *Camelot*, the long-running Broadway musical about King Arthur's Knights of the Round Table. It ended with the following verse: "Never let it be forgot, that once there was a spot, for one brief shining moment that was known as Camelot."

"There'll be great presidents again," Jackie told White, "but they'll never be another Camelot."[445] Henceforth for decades, the Kennedy presidency bore the moniker "Camelot."

Simultaneously, Jackie was working on reuniting Patrick and Arabella with their father. "I'll bring them together now," she told Dave Powers on the flight back from Dallas, and that's precisely what she set out to do. Within days, exhumation orders were issued as Cardinal Cushing, Frank Morrissey, Teddy Kennedy, and "Mummy" rallied, each assuming a role in reuniting Jack with his children.

In the darkness of the early night and behind Arlington's locked gates, Jackie, her sister Lee, Bobby, Ted and Joan Kennedy, and Patricia Kennedy Lawford gathered as Bishop Philip Hannan prayed and blessed the graves.

Jackie's still-born baby girl whom they named Arabella, was buried in the children's section of St. Columba's Cemetery in Middletown, Rhode Island, across the bay from Newport. She was buried with her dad in December of 1963, and the family donated her vacated grave to a priest.

Under the glow of the flickering flame Jackie had lit only nine days earlier, Patrick and Arabella were laid to rest, one on each side of their father.

Filled with doubts and recriminations of faith and life—and how could she not be—she reproached God. "I am trying to make my peace with God," she wrote Father Leonard. "I am so bitter against God…I think God must have taken Jack to show the world how lost we would be without him…a strange way of thinking to me and God will have some explaining to do to me, if I ever see him. But I promise you, I won't be bitter or bring up my children in a bitter way…I have to think there is a God, or I have no hope of finding Jack again…If I am mad at God, at least I love you who are His servant…And if you pray and I do too, maybe I will change, I will try."[446]

The original grave of Patrick Bouvier Kennedy in Brookline, Massachusetts. He too was exhumed in December 1963 and reinterred with his dad just days after his father was buried.

In the JFK Memorial Issue of *Look* Magazine in November 1964, Jackie made her last public comments regarding Jack's death. "Now I think I should have known that he was magic all along…I did know it, but I should have guessed that it could not last. I should have known that it was asking too much to dream that I might have grown old with him and see our children grow up together…He is free and we must live. Those who love him most know that 'the death you have dealt is more than the death which has swallowed you.'"

It was late in 1981, and Jackie was strolling down a New York street, following lunch with author Edward Klein. She was editing one of Klein's novels, and as they walked together, the conversation turned to her children. Caroline was working at the Metropolitan Museum of Art and sharing a West Side apartment with two roommates, and John was in his junior year at Brown University. "What do you tell your children about the relationship between you and President Kennedy?" Klein asked her.

"I'd rather not think about the past," she responded. "Please, let's not talk about the past," she added as if for emphasis. "I have to remain alive for myself. I don't want to dredge up the past."[447]

All that Jackie had become as first lady (the elegance, the grace, the style) and all that she had become as a widow (the personification of dignity, courage, and strength) ultimately grew into America's manifestation of its own grief and the world's symbol of its own pain.

Jackie had to leave her past behind, for it was her only chance to grasp the now. "She never wanted public notice," said Ted Kennedy at her eulogy. "In part, I think, because it brought back painful memories of unbearable sorrow endured in the glare of a million lights."

She would leave behind Hyannis Port and Hammersmith Farm, both vessels of her painful past, replacing them in 1978 with the purchase of a four-hundred-acre estate on Martha's Vineyard, where her penchant for both privacy and the sea were satisfied. And where there were no reminders of what once was, only memories to be made. Today it belongs to Caroline and her family, with its cauldron of yesterdays shared with her mother, her husband, and her children.

"Whenever you drive from the bridge from Washington into Virginia," Jackie told Teddy White, "you see the Lee mansion on the side of the hill in the distance. When Caroline was very little, the mansion was one of the first things she learned to recognize. Now at night, you can see his flame beneath the mansion, from miles away."[448]

Today she has found Jack again, and together they sleep with Patrick and Arabella beneath "his flame," which she lit more than fifty autumns ago, having graced the history of her country and the lives of those who loved her.

And on the shores of Narragansett Bay, across the emerald lawn of Hammersmith Farm, the sea still kisses the sand. If you pause and listen closely,

Arlington today. When Jackie first visited Arlington she was 11 years old and the Tomb of the Unknown Soldier held but one, fallen from World War I. Today she rests beneath the flame she herself lit on November 25, 1963, her son's third birthday, with Jack, Patrick and Arabella.

you will hear the whispers of an autumn long ago. Long before Camelot, and long before Jack. They're the whispers of a thirteen-year-old girl, following her first summer of "looking at the bay and drinking in the beauty."

I love the Autumn,
And yet I cannot say
All the thoughts and things
That make one feel this way.

I love walking on the angry shore,
To watch the angry sea;
Where summer people were before,
But now there's only me.

I love wood fires at night
That have a ruddy glow.
I stare at the flames
And think of long ago.

I love the feeling down inside me
That says to run away
To come and be a gypsy
And laugh the gypsy way.

Turtle neck sweaters—autumn fires
Swirling leaves and the sky
Riding my horse along the hills
To say a last goodbye.

The tangy taste of apples,
The snowy mist at morn,
The wanderlust inside you
When you hear the huntsman's horn.

Nostalgia—that's the Autumn
Dreaming through September
Just a million lovely things
I will always remember.

—*Jacqueline Bouvier*[449]

# Acknowledgments

It all begins with Laurie Austin of the JFK/Harry Truman Libraries. I am forever in your debt, for the door never opens without you, and for that I am eternally grateful.

I also want to thank William Manchester for writing the exhaustive chronology of *The Death of a President*. You will be happy to know, sir, that your painstaking chronicle holds up a half century later and you've done your nation a great service.

Sally Beddle Smith and Sarah Bradford, your outstanding detailed accounts of Jackie's magnificent life stand as true labors of love, thank you.

To the staff at the JFK Library: Abigail Malangone, Stacey Chandler, Michael Desmond and James Hill in research, and Maryrose Grossman in photo archives, your never ending capacity to help is greatly appreciated. James, thanks for going above and beyond. I never go there where I do not think I've arrived back home.

Stephen Fagin, museum curator at the Sixth Floor Museum in Dallas, offers a great perspective, bringing understanding and depth to, in the words of a Dallas newsman, "a tragedy that should never have happened."

Archivist and librarian Krishna Shenoy and assistant Marj Atkinson—your efforts opened new avenues of understanding for which I am grateful.

To Shane Dugger and Peter Martin, thanks for sharing.

For my sounding board: Paula, Lynda, Margeaux, Jules, Beth, Angela and Rachael, your input kept me energized and focused.

Thanks to the Cappellinis all, for the home I find when home to work, as well as the staff at the Hanson Public Library in Hanson, Massachusetts, where many words were found.

To my eight little nuggets who have blessed me and are constant reminders of the true purpose of it all.

Katie O'Dell at Globe Pequot, your confidence gave me confidence, and Jamie Muehl, Kristen Mellitt and the editorial staff, you made the finished product better.

And last and most, Jacqueline Lee Bouvier Kennedy Onassis, you were a true American hero, thank you for your service!

# Endnotes

1. Sarah Bradford, *America's Queen: The Life of Jacqueline Kennedy Onassis* (New York: Penguin Books, 2001): 18.
2. *Newport Mercury News,* August 21, 1897, 1.
3. Mary Van Rensselaer Thayer, *Jacqueline Bouvier Kennedy* (Garden City, NY: Doubleday and Company, 1961): 26.
4. Thayer, *Jacqueline Bouvier Kennedy*, 60.
5. *Ibid.*
6. *Ibid.*, 63.
7. Christopher Anderson, *Jack and Jackie: Portrait of an American Marriage* (New York: Avon Books, 1997): 70.
8. Interview, *Secret Lives of Jackie.* Executive Producer George Carey, Producer Charles Furneaux; a Barclay Carey Production for Channel Four and Discovery Communications 1995.
9. Anderson, *Jack and Jackie,* 71.
10. *Ibid.*
11. Bradford, *America's Queen,* 33.
12. *Ibid.*, 34.
13. *New York Daily News,* August 8, 1947, 3.
14. *Ibid.*, 53.
15. Cholly Knickerbocker, *San Francisco Examiner,* January 15, 1947, 19.
16. Bradford, *America's Queen,* 34.
17. Interview, *Secret Lives of Jackie.*
18. Bradford, *America's Queen,* 35.
19. Charles Bartlett, Oral History, JFK Library, Boston, MA.

[20] Anderson, *Jack and Jackie,* 84.
[21] Matt Viser, *Boston Globe,* May 13, 2014.
[22] Bartlett, Oral History.
[23] Edward Klein, *All Too Human: The Love Story of Jack and Jackie Kennedy* (New York: Pocket Books, 1997): 70.
[24] The decade of the 1950s saw American women marry younger than in any other decade of the twentieth century. U.S. Census Bureau.
[25] *Newport Daily News,* March 22, 1952, 2.
[26] Thayer, *Jacqueline Bouvier Kennedy*, 95.
[27] Michael Parsons, *Irish Times,* May 13, 2014.
[28] Sir Winston Churchill (1874–1965), a British politician, statesman, army officer, and writer, served twice as prime minister of the United Kingdom, from 1940 to 1945 and again from 1951 to 1955.
[29] George Byron (1788–1824), nobleman, politician, and poet, was widely regarded as one of Britain's greatest poets and leader of the Romantic movement in literature. Known for scurrilous affairs, he was deemed "mad, bad and dangerous to know" by Lady Caroline Lamb, a gothic novelist and one of Byron's paramours. Ironically, Byron's father was known as Captain John "Mad Jack" Byron.
[30] Anderson, *Jack and Jackie,* 87.
[31] Bradford, *America's Queen*, 58.
[32] Bartlett, Oral History.
[33] Noel Coward (1899–1973) was a prolific English playwright, composer, director, actor, and singer.
[34] Geoffrey Chaucer (1343–1400) was considered Britain's greatest poet of the Middle Ages.
[35] C. David Heymann, *A Woman Named Jackie: An Intimate Biography of Jacqueline Bouvier Kennedy Onassis* (Lyle Stuart, 2000), 121.
[36] Thayer, *Jacqueline Bouvier Kennedy,* 92.
[37] Viser, *Boston Globe.*
[38] *Newport Daily News,* June 25, 1953, 1.
[39] Thayer, *Jacqueline Bouvier Kennedy,* 36.
[40] Heymann, *Woman Named Jackie*, 127.
[41] Paul "Red" Fay first met Jack Kennedy at a PT boat training center in Melville, Rhode Island, in 1942. An usher in the wedding, he became Jack's under secretary of the navy. Their similar Irish Catholic backgrounds provided a springboard to a lasting friendship. He and his bride, Anita, were close companions to Jack and Jackie.
[42] Heymann, *Woman Named Jackie*, 126.
[43] Interview, Charles Whitehouse, *Secret Lives of Jackie Kennedy.*

44. Emily Post, *Etiquette in Society, in Business, in Politics and at Home* (New York: Funk & Wagnalls Company, 1922).
45. Interview, Red Fay, *Secret Lives of Jackie Kennedy.*
46. *Newport Daily News,* September 12, 1953, 1.
47. Bradford*, America's Queen,* 71.
48. Interview, Charles Spaulding, *Secret Lives of Jackie Kennedy.*
49. Heymann, *Woman Named Jackie*, 130.
50. Bradford, *America's Queen,* 72.
51. Interview, Spaulding.
52. Heymann, *Woman Named Jackie*, 133.
53. Jacqueline Kennedy, *Historic Conversations on Life with John F. Kennedy* (New York: Hyperion, 2011): 14.
54. *Ibid*., 13.
55. *Ibid*., 14.
56. Caroline Kennedy, *The Best-Loved Poems of Jacqueline Kennedy Onassis* (New York: Hyperion, 2005): 170.
57. Kennedy, *Historic Conversations,* 14.
58. Jack was diagnosed with Addison's disease in 1947, and it was hidden from the public throughout his life. LBJ leaked it to the press during the 1960 primary campaign, but it was successfully denied and warded off. His back injuries were also exacerbated, and in all likelihood caused, by the steroid regimen taken to combat colitis and Addison's.
59. Kennedy, *Historic Conversations*, 16.
60. *Ibid.,* 19.
61. *Ibid*., 18.
62. *Ibid.*
63. Robert Dallek, *An Unfinished Life: John F. Kennedy. 1917–1963* (Boston: Back Bay Books, 2004): 208.
64. Heymann, *Woman Named Jackie*, 193.
65. Kennedy, *Historic Conversations,* 35.
66. Heymann, *Woman Named Jackie*, 200.
67. Graeme Edge, "Threshold of a Dream" lyrics.
68. Heymann, *Woman Named Jackie*, 201.
69. Kenny O'Donnell (1924–1977) was a college roommate of Bobby Kennedy's at Harvard. He was with Jack from his first run for Congress. He became an integral part of the 1952 Senate campaign and became Jack's appointment secretary in the White House.
70. David Powers (1912–1998) was another member of the "Irish mafia." Dave was with Jack from the beginning, becoming one of his closest and most trusted friends.

A lynchpin in every campaign, he became special assistant to the president and was the first curator of the JFK Library.

71. Arthur Schlesinger (1917–2007) was a Harvard graduate. He later served as a history professor there as well. He joined the Kennedy administration as special assistant. He wrote one of the first biographies of Jack's administration and conducted hours of taped conversations with Jackie, which were released in 2011.

72. John Kenneth Galbraith (1908–2006) was another Harvard man who served as Jack's ambassador to India.

73. Kennedy, *Historic Conversations,* 22.

74. The Auchincloss Papers, JFK Library, Boston, MA.

75. Janet Auchincloss, Oral History, JFK Library, Boston, MA.

76. "Poetry and Power: Robert Frost's Inaugural Reading," poets.org.

77. *Ibid.*

78. Interview Robert Frost, NBC News, 1952.

79. "Poetry and Power."

80. Raymond Sinibaldi, *John F. Kennedy in New England* (Mount Pleasant, SC: Arcadia Publishing, 2017): 91.

81. "Poetry and Power."

82. *Ibid.*

83. Douglas Cater, "The Kennedy Look in the Arts," *Horizon* IV, no. 1 (September 1961).

84. Anderson, *Jack and Jackie,* 321.

85. Letitia Baldridge, *In the Kennedy Style* (New York: Doubleday, 1998): 36.

86. *New York Daily News,* April 8, 1961, 248.

87. Kennedy, *Historic Conversations,* 222.

88. *Philadelphia Inquirer,* April 4, 1961, 3.

89. Gwen Gibson, *New York Daily News*, April 8, 1961, 248.

90. *Ibid.*

91. Kennedy, *Historic Conversations,* 182, 183.

92. *Newport Daily News,* May 19, 1961, 1.

93. *Sydney Morning Herald,* May 21, 1961, 90.

94. Sally Bedell Smith, *Grace and Power: The Private World of the Kennedy White House* (New York: Random House, 2004): 197.

95. Baldridge, *Kennedy Style,* 37.

96. Bruce Phillips, *Ottawa Citizen,* May 17, 1961, 19.

97. Gordon Dewar, *Ottawa Journal,* May 17, 1961, 32.

98. Jean Robbie, *Ottawa Citizen,* May 17, 1961, 19.

99. *Daily Register,* May 18, 1961, 8.

100. *Newport Daily News,* May 18, 1961, 20.

101. Kennedy, *Historic Conversations,* 221.
102. Baldridge, Oral History.
103. Movietone newsreel.
104. *New York Daily News,* May 31, 1961, 3.
105. *Philadelphia Inquirer,* May 31, 1961, 2.
106. Merriman Smith, *Daily News Texan,* May 31, 1961, 1.
107. Baldridge, *Kennedy Style*, 39.
108. *Ibid.*
109. Baldridge, Oral History.
110. Antoinette Bradlee, *Boston Globe,* May 31, 1961, 1.
111. *Time,* June 9, 1961, 13.
112. Kennedy, *Historic Conversations,* 222, 223.
113. *Time,* June 9, 1961, 13.
114. Kennedy, *Historic Conversations,* 223, 224.
115. Smith, *Grace and Power*, 205.
116. *Boston Globe,* May 31, 1961, 18.
117. Baldridge, *Kennedy Style*, 39.
118. Smith, *Grace and Power*, 207.
119. *Ibid.*
120. *Ibid.,* 208.
121. Bud Abbott and Lou Costello were an American comedy team that started in burlesque, moved to radio, and then to television, along with making thirty-nine movies. Their baseball routine "Who's on First" was ranked by *Time* magazine as the number one comedy bit of the twentieth century. It plays on a continual loop at the Major League Baseball Hall of Fame in Cooperstown, New York.
122. Kennedy, *Historic Conversations,* 206, 207, 209.
123. Mary McGrory, *Boston Globe,* June 5, 1961, 11.
124. Baldridge, Oral History.
125. McGrory, *Boston Globe,* 11.
126. Kennedy, *Historic Conversations,* 207, 209.
127. Bill Adler, *The Eloquent Jacqueline Kennedy Onassis: A Portrait in Her Own Words* (New York: William Morrow, 2004): 146, 147.
128. *Baltimore Sun,* June 6, 1961, 1.
129. *San Mateo Times,* June 4, 1961, 1.
130. Bradlee, *Boston Globe.*
131. *Tampa Tribune,* May 3, 1961, 1.
132. *Daily News Texan,* May 31, 1961, 1.
133. *Baltimore Sun,* June 4, 1961, 1.
134. *El Paso Times,* June 4, 1961, 1.
135. *Oklahoman,* June 4, 1961, 1.

136. *Racine Journal Times,* June 4, 1961, 1.
137. Bradford, *American Queen*, 200.
138. *Ibid.*, 201.
139. Baldridge, Oral History.
140. Baldridge, *Kennedy Style*, 49.
141. Kenneth O'Donnell and David Powers, *Johnny We Hardly Knew Ye* (New York: Little, Brown and Company, 1972): 269.
142. Smith, *Grace and Power*, 216.
143. *Ibid.*
144. *Ibid.,* 217.
145. Baldridge, *Kennedy Style*, 49.
146. *Ibid.*, 50.
147. *Ibid.*
148. *Ibid.*, 52.
149. *Baltimore Sun,* July 12, 1961, 1.
150. Baldridge, *Kennedy Style*, 55.
151. Baldridge, Oral History.
152. *Ibid.*
153. Stuart married Eleanor Calvert Custiss, the widow of Washington's stepson John Parke Custiss, in 1783. He also served as an elector from Virginia in the first presidential election, casting one of his two votes for Washington. President Washington appointed him one of the three commissioners to oversee the surveying of the Federal City, which they named the "City of Washington" in "The Territory of Columbia."
154. George Washington Letter to David Stuart, June 15, 1790, https://founders.archives.gov/documents/Washington/05-05-02-0334.
155. *Baltimore Sun,* July 12, 1961, 1.
156. Clint Hill, *Mrs. Kennedy and Me* (New York: Gallery Books, 2012): 101.
157. Auchincloss Papers, JFK Library, Boston, MA.
158. The biography of the eighteenth-century French statesman, bishop, politician, diplomat, and rogue, who survived five French regimes.
159. Hill, *Mrs. Kennedy and Me,* 102.
160. Dave Kindred, "From Jackie to JFK," *Golf Digest,* November 20, 2013.
161. Auchincloss Papers.
162. *Ibid.*
163. *Ibid.*
164. Arthur Schlesinger Jr., *A Thousand Days: John F. Kennedy in the White House* (New York: Mariner Books, 2002): 524.
165. Kennedy, *Historic Conversations,* 239.
166. *Ibid.*

167. Kirk Lemoyne Billings, Oral History, JFK Library, Boston, MA.
168. Kennedy, *Historic Conversations,* 209.
169. Bradford, *America's Queen,* 216.
170. Kennedy, *Historic Conversations,* 239
171. Billings, Oral History.
172. Kennedy, *Historic Conversations,* 240.
173. *Ibid.*, 241.
174. *Ibid.*, 243.
175. *Ibid.*, 245.
176. *Newport Daily News,* May 8, 1962, 1.
177. *Ibid.*, May 11, 1962, 1.
178. *Ibid.,* August 9, 1962, 1.
179. *Ibid.,* September 1, 1962, 4.
180. Bradford, *America's Queen,* 234.
181. *Ibid.*, 218.
182. Smith, *Grace and Power*, 261.
183. *Newport Daily News,* March 23, 1962, 1.
184. Smith, *Grace and Power*, 382.
185. Auchincloss Papers.
186. Maxwell Anderson, "September Song" lyrics.
187. Smith, *Grace and Power*, 399.
188. *Ibid.*
189. Ben Bradlee, *Conversations with Kennedy* (New York: W.W. Norton and Company, 1984): 198.
190. *Ibid.*, 199.
191. Janet Auchincloss, Oral History.
192. *Ibid.*
193. Randy Taraborrelli, *Janet, Jackie and Lee: The Secret Lives of Janet Auchincloss and Her Daughters Jackie Kennedy Onassis and Lee Radziwill* (New York: St. Martin's Press, 2018): 177.
194. Bradlee, *Conversations with Kennedy*, 200.
195. *Ibid.*, 202.
196. Janet Auchincloss, Oral History.
197. *Newport Daily News,* September 13, 1963, 1.
198. Hill, *Mrs. Kennedy and Me,* 264.
199. Jack became interested in James Bond novels in 1955, when recuperating from back surgery. Newport resident Marion "Oatsie" Leiter-Charles visited him and brought along a copy of Ian Fleming's *Casino Royale.* Jack was hooked, and in fact James Bond novels were the only fiction he read. Oatsie introduced Ian Fleming and Jack in 1960, and Fleming referenced him in future novels.

200. Ralph Martin, *A Hero for Our Time: An Intimate Story of the Kennedy Years* (N.p.: Fawcett Crest, 1984): 545.
201. Gerald Blaine, *The Kennedy Detail: JFK's Secret Service Agents Break Their Silence* (New York: Gallery Books, 2011): 130.
202. *Ibid*., 131, 132.
203. Thurston Clark, *JFK'S Last Hundred Days: The Transformation of a Man and the Emergence of a President* (New York: Penguin, 2013): 185.
204. Smith, *Grace and Power*, 409.
205. "Kennedy Played His Death for Home Movie," *New York Times,* August 14, 1983.
206. *Newport Mercury News,* November 1, 1963, 1.
207. Klein*, All Too Human*, 342.
208. *Ibid.*
209. William Manchester, *Death of a President* (Boston: Back Bay Books, 2013): 67.
210. Blaine, *Kennedy Detail*, 26–27.
211. Pamela Turnure, Oral History, JFK Library, Boston, MA.
212. Hill*, Mrs. Kennedy and Me*, 241.
213. *Ibid.,* 242.
214. Dr. Roy Heffernan, Oral History, JFK Library, Boston, MA.
215. Lawrence K. Altman MD, "A Kennedy Baby's Life," *New York Times,* July 29, 2013.
216. *Newport Daily News,* August 7, 1963.
217. Janet Auchincloss, Oral History.
218. O'Donnell and Powers, *Johnny We Hardly Knew Ye*, 377.
219. *Ibid*., 377.
220. *Ibid*., 378.
221. Hill, *Mrs. Kennedy and Me*, 245.
222. Francis Morrissey, Oral History, JFK Library, Boston, MA.
223. Lemoyne Billings, Oral History, JFK Library, Boston, MA.
224. *Ibid.*
225. *Ibid.*
226. Klein*, All Too Human*, 215.
227. Hill, *Mrs. Kennedy and Me*, 246.
228. Kennedy, *Historic Conversations.*
229. Richard Cardinal Cushing, Oral History, JFK Library, Boston, MA.
230. Blaine, *Kennedy Detail*, 128.
231. David Ormsby Gore, Oral History, JFK Library, Boston, MA.
232. Janet Auchincloss, Oral History.
233. *Newport Daily News,* August 12, 1963.
234. Barbara Lemming, *Jacqueline Bouvier Kennedy Onassis: The Untold Story* (New York: St. Martins Griffen, 2015): 120.

235. Hill, *Mrs. Kennedy and Me*, 248.
236. Nancy Tuckerman, Oral History, JFK Library, Boston, MA.
237. Turnure, Oral History.
238. Paul Fay, Oral History, JFK Library, Boston, MA.
239. James Reed, Oral History, JFK Library, Boston, MA.
240. Martin, *Hero for Our Time*, 528.
241. *Ibid.,* 528.
242. *Ibid.,* 529.
243. Klein, *All Too Human,* 333.
244. Edward Kennedy, *True Compass: A Memoir* (New York: Twelve, 2009): 199.
245. Manchester, *Death of a President,* 70.
246. "Interview JFK The Final Hours," *National Geographic,* 2013.
247. Manchester, *Death of a President,* 76
248. "Final Hours."
249. Tuckerman, Oral History.
250. "Final Hours."
251. *Ibid.*
252. O'Donnell and Powers, *Johnny We Hardly Knew Ye*, 22.
253. Lady Bird Johnson, Oral History, LBJ Library, Austin, TX.
254. "Final Hours."
255. Manchester, *Death of a President,* 84.
256. *Ibid.*, 85.
257. "Final Hours."
258. Manchester, *Death of a President,* 87.
259. "Final Hours."
260. Peter Lisagor, *Chicago Daily News,* November 22, 1963, 1.
261. Manchester, *Death of a President,* 87.
262. *Ibid.*
263. Edward Klein, *Just Jackie: Her Private Years* (New York: Ballantine Books, 1998): 10.
264. "Final Hours."
265. Manchester, *Death of a President*, 112.
266. *Ibid*.
267. *JFK: A Time Remembered,* anniversary documentary; 1988.
268. Klein, *Just Jackie,* 11.
269. "Final Hours."
270. *Ibid.*
271. *Ibid.*
272. *Ibid.*
273. KTVT Television news footage.

274. Clint Hill, *Five Days in November* (New York: Gallery Books, 2013): 78–79.
275. KTVT.
276. "Final Hours."
277. Hill, *Five Days*, 72.
278. "Final Hours."
279. *Ibid.*
280. Manchester, *Death of a President,* 118.
281. "Final Hours."
282. Manchester, *Death of a President,* 120.
283. O'Donnell and Powers, *Johnny We Hardly Knew Ye*, 24.
284. Manchester, *Death of a President,* 121.
285. Nicola Langford, *Hotel Texas, An Art Exhibition for the President and Mrs. John F. Kennedy.*
286. *Ibid.,* 57.
287. Manchester, *Death of a President,* 121.
288. *Ibid.*
289. O'Donnell and Powers, *Johnny We Hardly Knew Ye*, 25.
290. "Final Hours."
291. *Ibid.*
292. *Ibid.*
293. "Personal Moments Lasting Impressions," *USA Today,* October 28, 2013.
294. John Byrne, Oral History, JFK Library, Boston, MA.
295. Manchester, *Death of a President,* 127.
296. O'Donnell and Powers, *Johnny We Hardly Knew Ye*, 26.
297. Manchester, *Death of a President,* 131.
298. Klein*, All Too Human*, 344.
299. Manchester, *Death of a President,* 152.
300. *Ibid.,* 136.
301. John Connally Interview with Gordon Wilkison, KTBC Television, Austin, Texas.
302. James Wright, Oral History, Sixth Floor Museum, 1996.
303. O'Donnell and Powers, *Johnny We Hardly Knew Ye*, 26.
304. Warren Commission Testimony, Jacqueline Kennedy.
305. Dr. Toni Glover, Oral History, Sixth Floor Museum, 2013.
306. Clint Hill Interview, C-Span, 2010.
307. Manchester, *Death of a President,* 152.
308. Kenneth O'Donnell Interview, 1973, https://www.youtube.com/watch?v=-c6RtfEX0Cw.
309. Manchester, *Death of a President,* 154.
310. Hill Interview, C-Span.

311. Wright, Oral History.
312. John Connally Interview, NBC, youtube.com/watch?v=4svgOqQmS3o.
313. Warren Commission Testimony, Jacqueline Kennedy.
314. Warren Commission Testimony, Clint Hill.
315. Warren Commission Testimony of Mrs. John B. (Nellis) Connally.
316. Glover, Oral History.
317. Manchester, *Death of a President,* 170.
318. Hill, *Mrs. Kennedy and Me,* 293.
319. Manchester, *Death of a President,* 171.
320. *Ibid.,* 172.
321. Wright, Oral History.
322. Byrne, Oral History.
323. Dr. Marion Jenkins, Parkland chief anesthesiologist, November 22, 1963, Symposium, youtube.com/watch?v=DX58vrL5ZiA&t=294s; youtube.com/watch?v=KwKXBiYWweA.
324. *Ibid.*
325. Manchester, *Death of a President,* 186.
326. *Ibid.,* 188.
327. Klein, *All Too Human*, 346.
328. Interview Father Oscar Huber, https://www.youtube.com/watch?v=tqtssPUmFT4.
329. Manchester, *Death of a President,* 218.
330. Hill, *Mrs. Kennedy and Me,* 296.
331. Oscar Huber, Folder, JFK Library, Boston, MA.
332. Huber, Interview.
333. Manchester, *Death of a President,* 289, 290, 293, 294, 295, 296, 297, 302, 303, 304.
334. Hill, *Mrs. Kennedy and Me,* 300.
335. Manchester, *Death of a President,* 306.
336. *Ibid.,* 308.
337. Diary, Lady Bird Johnson, LBJ Library, Austin, TX.
338. *Ibid.*
339. Manchester, *Death of a President,* 317.
340. Turnure, Oral History.
341. Manchester, *Death of a President,* 326, 327.
342. Merriman Smith, "Four Days That Shocked the World," Colpix Records.
343. Sid Davis, Oral History, LBJ Library, Austin, TX.
344. Manchester, *Death of a President,* 327.
345. *Ibid.,* 347.
346. O'Donnell and Powers, *Johnny We Hardly Knew Ye*, 39.
347. Manchester, *Death of a President,* 348.

348. *Ibid.,* 349.
349. *Ibid.,* 348.
350. Interview Dave Powers, 1988, https://www.youtube.com/watch?v=sZ1Qo2JVEe4.
351. Manchester, *Death of a President,* 350, 351.
352. Hill, *Five Days*, 125.
353. Hill, *Mrs. Kennedy and Me*, 302, 303.
354. O'Donnell and Powers, *Johnny We Hardly Knew Ye*, 378.
355. *Ibid*., 379.
356. *Ibid.,* 39.
357. Mary Barelli Gallagher, *My Life with Jacqueline Kennedy* (N.p.: David McKay, 1969): 325.
358. Manchester, *Death of a President, 348.*
359. Ibid.
360. Hill, *Five Days,* 127.
361. Lemming, *Jacqueline Bouvier Kennedy Onassis*, 133.
362. Manchester, *Death of a President,* 390.
363. *A Time Remembered.*
364. Manchester, *Death of a President,* 406, 407, 415, 416, 417, 418.
365. William Walton, Oral History, JFK Library, Boston, MA.
366. Manchester, *Death of a President,* 428.
367. *Ibid.*
368. NBC News Footage, https://www.youtube.com/watch?v=u-PfYnUJ2Ek.
369. Tuckerman, Oral History.
370. Manchester, *Death of a President,* 428.
371. *Ibid.,* 429.
372. Tuckerman, Oral History.
373. Manchester, *Death of a President,* 432.
374. *Ibid.,* 435.
375. Auchincloss, Oral History.
376. Manchester, *Death of a President,* 452.
377. *Ibid.,* 452, 463, 464, 485, 486.
378. Hill, *Five Days*, 176.
379. Hill, *Mrs. Kennedy and Me*, 314.
380. *Ibid.,* 315.
381. Manchester, *Death of a President,* 490.
382. Now named the Jacqueline Kennedy Garden.
383. Bishop Philip Hannan would return to Arlington and pray over the graves of Arabella and Patrick when they were interred next to their father in December 1963, Robert Kennedy in 1968 and Jackie herself in 1994.

384. Manchester, *Death of a President*, 507.
385. Manchester, *Death of a President,* 495, 496, 510, 516, 517.
386. Hill, *Five Days*, 160.
387. Hill, *Mrs. Kennedy and Me,* 311.
388. Manchester, *Death of a President,* 517, 518.
389. *Ibid.*, 540.
390. Manchester, *Death of a President,* 541, 543, 546, 550.
391. Stuart Loory, *Boston Globe,* November 25, 1963, 4.
392. Manchester, *Death of a President,* 574.
393. *Ibid.*, 577.
394. *Ibid.*, 580.
395. Kennedy, *Historic Conversations*, 53.
396. *Ibid.*, 54.
397. Manchester, *Death of a President*, 580.
398. *Sydney Morning Herald,* November 27, 1963, 1.
399. *Montreal Gazette,* November 26, 1963, 1.
400. *Guardian,* November 26, 1963, 18
401. *Pittsburg Press,* November 26, 1963, 22.
402. *Boston Globe,* November 26, 1963, 1.
403. *Newport Daily News,* November 26, 1963, 1.
404. Jerry Van De Heuvel, *New York Post,* November 26, 1963, 3.
405. Robert Donovan, *Los Angeles Times,* Final Edition, November 25, 1963, 1.
406. Helen Thomas, *Tampa Tribune,* November 26, 1963, 1.
407. *Honolulu Advertiser,* November 26, 1963, 1.
408. *Hays Daily News,* November 26, 1963, 1.
409. Manchester, *Death of a President*, 580.
410. Martin Luther King Jr., "I Have a Dream," National Archives, Washington, D.C.
411. *Alabama Journal,* November 27, 1963, 4.
412. Manchester, *Death of a President*, 582.
413. CBS News footage.
414. Manchester, *Death of a President*, 589.
415. Kennedy, *Historic Conversations*, 104.
416. Manchester, *Death of a President*, 589.
417. *Ibid.*
418. *Ibid.*, 590.
419. CBS News footage.
420. Manchester, *Death of a President*, 601.
421. CBS News footage.
422. Manchester, *Death of a President*, 602.
423. *Ibid.*

424. CNN News footage, Edward Kennedy Eulogy for Jacqueline Kennedy, May 1994.
425. Manchester, *Death of a President*, 606.
426. *Ibid.*, 607.
427. McGeorge Bundy, Oral History, JFK Library, Boston, MA.
428. Manchester, *Death of a President*, 608.
429. *Ibid.*, 611.
430. *Ibid.*, 609.
431. *Ibid.*
432. Angier Biddle Duke, Oral History, JFK Library, Boston, MA.
433. Interview Angier Biddle Duke, *A Time Remembered.*
434. Manchester, *Death of a President*, 610.
435. Duke, Oral History.
436. Manchester, *Death of a President*, 610.
437. Hill, *Five Days*, 228, 229.
438. Manchester, *Death of a President*, 615.
439. *Ibid.*, 616.
440. Interview William Venden Hueval, *A Time Remembered.*
441. Manchester, *Death of a President*, 617.
442. *Ibid.*, 618.
443. *Ibid.*, 619.
444. Hill, *Mrs. Kennedy and Me*, 322.
445. *Life,* December 7, 1963.
446. Matt Viser, *Boston Globe,* May 13, 2014.
447. Klein, *All Too Human*, 6.
448. *Life.*
449. Kennedy, *Best-Loved Poems*, 170.

# Index